# WITH ALL DUE RESPECT

## Keys for Building Effective School Discipline

### Ronald G. Morrish

purposeful design®
publications
A Division of ACSI

Colorado Springs, Colorado

A Division of ACSI

Books, Textbooks, and Educational Resources
for Christian Educators and Schools Worldwide

Purposeful Design Publications is the publishing division of the Association of Christian Schools International (ACSI) and is committed to the ministry of Christian school education, to enable Christian educators and schools worldwide to effectively prepare students for life. As the publisher of books, textbooks, and other educational resources, Purposeful Design Publications strives to produce biblically sound materials that reflect Christian scholarship and stewardship and that address the identified needs of Christian schools around the world.

With All Due Respect: Keys for Building Effective School Discipline
Author:  Ronald G. Morrish
Editor:  Gina Brandon
Design:  Mike Riester
Cover Photos:  Ablestock.com


Printed in Canada
Publisher's Cataloguing-in-Publication Data
1. Discipline 2. School Discipline 3. Classroom Management
4. Teacher Training 5. Effective Schools

ISBN 1-58331-061-4                                        Catalog #6505
Purposeful Design Publications
A division of ACSI
PO Box 65130 · Colorado Springs, CO 80962-5130
http://www.acsi.org

*To Laure, my wife and best friend.*

*Her gift for teaching,*
*dedication to her students,*
*and commitment to discipline*
*have inspired many of*
*the principles espoused in this book.*

# Table of Contents

# Building School Discipline

# Applications

# Tip of the Week

# Recommended Reading

# Appendices

# Introduction

## Where Has All the Respect Gone?

If there is one issue that unites teachers and parents these days, it is the desire to improve discipline in our schools. Everyone wants to see more respect and responsibility from students, less disruption in classrooms, and an end to bullying.

Demands on teachers are escalating rapidly—new curricula, less preparation time, more meetings, and much more paperwork. It is impossible for teachers to meet these demands if their time must be spent dealing with disruption, defiance, and aggression. For teachers to provide high-quality lessons and meet the needs of individual students, it is essential for students to behave appropriately and show respect for the rights and needs of others.

Parents are equally concerned. They want to be able to send their children off to school without worrying about their safety. Parents have been shocked by the highly publicized rash of violent incidents in schools and stunned to learn that it could happen anywhere, anytime. They want gangs and weapons out of school.

Meeting these goals is an enormous challenge. Obviously, children do not develop positive behavior by accident. It is the result of great discipline—which brings us directly to the purpose of this book. We need to establish the keys for building effective discipline in our schools.

*With All Due Respect* provides these keys, but it does so with a unique perspective. Your journey through this book will force you to look, not just at your discipline strategies, but also at your beliefs regarding how we have been raising and teaching our children. As you will learn, your beliefs have a direct impact on the outcome of your strategies. These days, many people equate discipline with punishment and consequences, a simplistic view that has led to a widespread overreliance on punitive techniques. Somehow, we must find a way to reinstill the concept that discipline is mainly about teaching and training our children to be the kind of children we want them to be. This concept is not some new theory. The principles espoused have been followed by great teachers and parents for many years.

One of the great ironies about the discipline debate is that there are teachers who know, and have always known, how to solve the problem. They do it every day in their classrooms. You would think that we could just learn it from them, either by watching how they do it, or having them explain it to us. If only it were that simple.

Try to learn discipline from the "masters" and you will immediately run into two big problems. First, when discipline is done well, it is almost invisible. You cannot see it. It is not like poor discipline in which you can easily see all the punishments, detentions, confrontations, students in isolation, and so on. You can also hear the raised voices and feel the constant tension.

With effective discipline, all you see is students behaving well, doing their assignments, and getting along with each other. Lessons are relatively uninterrupted, and transitions are quick and smooth. When a problem does arise, it is dealt with quickly and quietly. Unfortunately, try as you might, you will not see how the teacher creates the effect. It almost seems to happen by itself.

The second problem is that great teachers are, without a shadow of a doubt, the worst people in the world for explaining to anyone else how they discipline their students. It is so natural and intuitive for them that they cannot put it into words. Obviously, if effective discipline cannot be learned from master teachers, then there is a very real danger of teachers being unduly influenced by every new theory that comes along.

In fact, this is exactly what has been happening over the years. Teachers have implemented trendy forms of discipline that do not get the job done. The only way of avoiding this situation is to analyze the discipline techniques used by effective teachers so they can be shared and duplicated.

That is what this book is all about—practical, common-sense concepts that we have lost sight of over the years. These principles were first described in the book *Secrets of Discipline: 12 Keys for Raising Responsible Children* (ISBN 0-9681131-0-9), which preceded the present text. It looked at issues that were common to parents and teachers.

*With All Due Respect* is specifically for educators. School issues need to be addressed separately because the learning environment is unique. It has its own special problems and demands. Parents, after all, are not required to keep large groups of children on task for five hours every day and to implement complex curricula, usually without adequate resources.

Schools work best when they operate as learning communities where everybody gets involved in a common effort to accomplish common goals. Hence, when you see the word *teacher* in this book, remember that it refers not only to the curriculum specialists in the classrooms, but also to the teaching assistants and childcare workers, the school administrators, secretaries, and caretaking staff—all of whom must work together. Unless everyone is on the same page, going in the same direction, we will not be successful in bringing respect back into our schools.

**Note:** Throughout this book, the pronoun he has been used in most descriptions of student behavior. This pronoun is not intended to imply that only males experience behavioral difficulties. All examples apply equally to both genders.

**Every new initiative adds to the workload ...**

but effective discipline is an investment.
The extra time and effort that it requires,
especially at the beginning of the school year,
is repaid many times over in the long run.

# CHAPTER ONE

# Not by Management Alone

# Not by Management Alone

*As an educator, you know that many students come
from homes where supervision and discipline are lax,
and from communities where social problems abound.*

*You know that regardless of these problems, it is essential
for students to behave appropriately in school. The ability
of teachers to deliver quality education depends on it.*

*And since you know such behavior doesn't happen by accident,
you understand the importance of providing
effective discipline within the school environment.*

So, let's get right to the point. For the past twenty years, teachers have consistently been taught to elicit positive student behavior by using a set of strategies known as "Classroom Management." These strategies are designed to keep students on task, minimize disruptions, and maintain general control of the learning environment. They have proven to be valuable techniques, and every teacher should be proficient in their use.

But, understand this: *Classroom management alone will not give you the kind of students you want.* If you are like most teachers, you have high expectations for students. It is not enough to simply have them quiet and on task. You also want them to be respectful, responsible and cooperative. You want students who can be trusted to behave well without direct supervision, to avoid conflict, and to make a positive contribution. *This requires* discipline ... *and there is more to discipline than just classroom management.*

Discipline is about developing and creating appropriate behaviors, not just managing the ones that are already there. It is about instilling values and positive attitudes, teaching appropriate social skills and training children how to work within a structure of rules and limits. Because it deals with all aspects of behavior, discipline is capable of producing higher order attributes such as respect and responsibility. This sounds great, but it is really a parental responsibility, right? Absolutely, up to a point.

We are actually talking about two different jobs here, so let's clear up any confusion. Parents are responsible for the overall positive development of their children. They are supposed to teach their children the skills and values necessary for success in the world at large. It would be neither appropriate, nor feasible, for teachers to assume this responsibility.

School discipline is a different issue. It involves teaching students to be respectful and responsible in school. That's all. If it so happens that the discipline used in school helps children deal positively with the world outside, that would be a bonus.

There are several reasons why it is important for teachers to take on this specific task. First, even if parents have done a good job with discipline, their efforts may not carry over to the school environment, especially when children have certain traits such as obstinacy or impulsivity. Second, in a multicultural world, teachers cannot be assured that the lessons taught in homes are the lessons needed for school. And finally, it will always be the case that some parents fail to provide their children with the necessary supervision and discipline. Teachers must at least provide enough within the school setting to protect the quality of the learning environment and the safety of staff and students—one of the great challenges. How is it possible to elicit appropriate behavior from students who have not had a solid foundation laid in the home environment?

### And the Award for Special Effects Goes to ...

To accomplish this goal, school discipline relies on a special effect. It takes advantage of the fact that behavior is, to a certain extent, situational. People are capable of learning behaviors that apply only to a specific place or occasion. Inappropriate behaviors are excluded. An excellent example is the behavior of people at church. When attending church, people act in a manner considered suitable for that environment, even if they would normally behave very differently. It does not matter if they are rich or poor, if the family has one parent or two, or how smart they may be. It is clearly understood that there is a correct way to behave at church. Negative behaviors such as rude language and provocative clothing are not allowed.

Within the school environment, effective discipline has exactly the same impact. As children arrive at school, they literally switch on the set of behaviors associated with being students. Clearly defining these expectations increases the effectiveness of the system, blocking out the negative behaviors and attitudes that children could bring with them from their home and community settings.

## Paying the Price

Classroom management does not create this effect—and classroom management is what most teachers rely on. Instead of creating a set of situational behaviors, classroom management operates on the premise that teachers can "manage" whatever behaviors the students bring with them. Teachers can do so, however, only if there is a high degree of consistency between school expectations and the community at large.

The system quickly breaks down if a significant number of students arrive at school with negative and antisocial behaviors. Allowing these behaviors into the school simply overwhelms the efforts of the teachers— and this is exactly what has been happening in many schools. Students have been bringing into school the constant banter, defiant attitudes, provocative language, and poor social skills that are commonplace in the outside world. These behaviors are incompatible with academic learning and interfere with the progress of other students. This situation is causing enormous headaches for teachers, especially since it is happening at a time when the demands on teachers are escalating at an extraordinary rate.

## Not Allowed in School

We will never have the kind of schools we desire if we continue to allow students to act as if school is nothing more than an extension of the outside community. Schools should be learning communities with their own standards and expectations for behavior.

This is not a new concept. There are already teachers who apply this principle. They refuse to accept "potluck" in terms of student behavior—to simply accept whatever behavior the students bring with them into the classroom. Instead, these teachers have their own vision of how they want their students to behave, and they teach them to act accordingly. The classroom door is their threshold. Beyond this point, only appropriate behavior is allowed.

The impact is nothing less than amazing. When students enter the classrooms of these teachers, they adopt an entirely different demeanor. Gone are the belligerence and hostility. In their place are courtesy, cooperation, and respect. Students would not even think about misbehaving in this classroom, not because harsh consequences have been threatened, but because the teacher has left no alternative other than to behave appropriately—what effective discipline is all about.

**One Is Not Enough**

However, having this effect occur in individual classrooms is no longer sufficient. With the pressure on today's schools, it is time to create this effect throughout the entire school environment. To accomplish this goal, every teacher in a school must be able to employ effective discipline techniques. Then, they must coordinate their efforts, working together to accomplish the task. *Classroom management you can do by yourself; school discipline must be done as a team.*

School discipline can only be done if all staff members are on the same page, going in the same direction. There must be a consensus about expectations for student behavior. There must also be a willingness to work together, to put aside some personal preferences, and to enforce common rules and standards.

**It Is a Lost Art**

Unfortunately, we are presently far away from any sense of teamwork in most schools. Thanks to twenty years of classroom management, we now have many teachers who think that discipline is a matter of what they personally do with their own students in their own classroom. As a result, there are more and more schools where all the teachers do "their own thing" regarding student behavior. Students lose their general sense of how they are supposed to behave in the school and are forced, instead, to learn each individual teacher's rules and expectations. Parents also struggle with trying to make sense of this inconsistent approach, and they frequently end up challenging individual teachers on the fairness of their rules and decisions.

That is not all. Because it is "classroom" management, many teachers now focus almost exclusively on the behavior of their own students. The misbehavior of students from other classrooms is perceived as being the responsibility of either the teachers of those students or the school administrators. In fact, we even have teachers who sincerely believe that how their students behave in somebody else's classroom has nothing to do with them.

They even believe that how their students behave for a substitute teacher is up to the sub! Consider the implications of this concept. Substitute teachers have, by definition, virtually no time to establish rapport with students, to learn special methods for dealing with specific students, or for following through on issues that arise during the day. Hence, the success of their efforts is highly dependent on the "regular" teacher who must set up the situation for success. As obvious as this may be, most substitute teachers are now expected to do their job in isolation. Welcome to the world of classroom management. It is time to reverse this trend and get discipline back on track. The only question is how?

## Charting a New Course

If effective school discipline is your goal, here is what it takes. First, on a personal level, you must expand your own repertoire of skills to include a full range of discipline techniques. Keep in mind that classroom management strategies are an integral part of discipline. Hence, the process is one of adding to present techniques, not discarding them. The second step is to deal with procedures for coordinating discipline across the school. Once all of these principles have been established, it is possible to look at the application of these strategies to specific situations and behaviors.

### Does It Make a Difference?

If you need proof that effective school discipline can have a dramatic impact, just look at the gains achieved by the educators at Almeria Middle School in Fontana, California. Located just outside of Los Angeles, the school has 1,600 students in grades six, seven, and eight. The community has a large Hispanic population that requires the school to deal with the accompanying issues of language and culture. In addition, the fact that a significant number of lower income families live in the community has implications in a wide variety of areas including childcare, nutrition, and financial support for school trips and events. All in all, it is fair to say that the teachers at Almeria Middle School are confronted with all of the problems that typify inner city schools in modern urban areas.

The teachers committed two days of their summer vacation to professional development workshops designed according to the principles in this book. They examined their discipline methods, coordinated their efforts, and developed implementation plans to prepare for the start of the new academic year. A series of follow-up sessions was also scheduled that would allow the teachers to evaluate and refine their efforts.

Here is what happened. In the first month of the new academic year, the school staff achieved an 85 percent drop in the number of discipline incidents significant enough to require administrative involvement. This improvement was maintained at 55 percent for the year as a whole. (Any new initiative naturally starts with a high level of intensity and then changes to a more sustainable level.)

Before we go any further, let's clarify one specific issue. This improvement in student behavior was not accomplished by simply suspending every student who misbehaved, a simplistic and politically popular process that is being considered, or adopted, in a number of jurisdictions. At Almeria, the number of suspensions dropped by 40 percent proving, once again, that it is rarely necessary to suspend well-disciplined students. During the follow-up evaluation, the teachers reported the following improvements:

- Students on task quicker
- No major events
- Fewer punishments
- Fewer office referrals by far
- More respect shown to staff and students
- Disrespectful students "stuck out"
- Quality of work improved
- Greater sense of common ground, teamwork among staff
- Teachers felt more authority, power, and competence

Would you like to see these improvements in your school? You bet! So, let's get started.

**Let's take a moment and give credit where credit is due.**

As research has consistently demonstrated, workshops do not change schools—teachers change schools. The success achieved at Almeria School was due entirely to the extraordinary dedication of its staff and their commitment to the implementation of positive discipline techniques. Credit also goes to Principal Richard Roth who provided the vision and leadership essential for all major school initiatives.

# CHAPTER TWO

# Lessons Along the Way

# Lessons Along the Way

*First, it is important to understand that discipline is trendy.*
*Every so often, certain techniques become highly popularized*
*and everyone jumps on the bandwagon. As with other trends,*
*the pendulum tends to swing from one extreme to the other.*

## Pendulum to the Right

Forty years ago, discipline meant obedience—a special form of obedience in which children were required to be passively submissive to authority. They were to do what they were told to do, with no discussion whatsoever. Their opinions were neither solicited nor respected.

If passive submission is the goal, then it is necessary to employ techniques related to intimidation, because intimidation is what creates the effect. We did. In schools, the strap was used to maintain "discipline." Not every student "got the strap," but every student knew it was there. The mere threat of receiving the strap kept everyone in line. Parents used similar techniques such as spankings and the belt. Other common strategies included the use of sarcasm and ridicule that were also intimidating.

A considerable number of people still support the use of these techniques, particularly because intimidation has a powerful, short-term impact. In the long term, however, these techniques can create a great deal of resentment and rebellion. Even forty years ago, most people were looking for positive alternatives. They were concerned that children were excessively passive and would even obey inappropriate commands. For instance, young children would get into a stranger's car when the stranger instructed them to. Another concern was that many adolescents rebelled against the excessive use of adult control.

## Pendulum to the Left

Society eventually changed and moved away from the use of physical force. Adults were advised to allow children to "express" themselves. Hostility and confrontation were healthy outlets for anger. Rudeness was a personal expression of the self.

The popular theory of the time was that if we just gave and gave to children without asking for anything back, and if we treated them like little adults, then they would appreciate the treatment and reciprocate. Although this theory may sound foolish, millions of parents accepted it, raised their children in a permissive environment, and ended up with spoiled brats. To the credit of teachers, most of them understood intuitively that this would not work in a school environment and avoided the trap.

## Pendulum to the Right

Unhappy with discipline techniques that created self-centered children, we then adopted behavioral principles developed during laboratory research into animal behavior, particularly rats that were trained in "Skinner boxes." Researchers confirmed that what occurs after a behavior is very important in the behavioral process. A behavior that is positively reinforced is more likely to occur in the future. A behavior that is punished or consequenced (negative reinforcement) is less likely to occur in the future. They also discovered that providing the reinforcement systematically in a program could dramatically increase its effectiveness. The researchers recommended the development of similar techniques for raising and teaching children. Since these concepts made good common sense, they were quickly accepted, and the age of behavior modification was born.

We told children what to do, and if they did it, we rewarded them, especially with praise. (The overwhelming majority of rewards and consequences are verbal, because they are quick and easy.) In addition to praise, we also used privileges, treats, points, stickers, and stars.

If children refused to do as they were told, then consequences were used, especially scolding (verbal). Other consequences included the use of time-outs, loss of privileges, loss of points, and so on.

Charts were frequently employed to ensure the rewards and consequences were applied systematically. However, it was not very long before most teachers and parents were expressing dissatisfaction with this approach. They found that behavior modification prevented them from being spontaneous with children. They also felt as if they were on the charts just as much as the children were. They felt behavior modification was too cold and impersonal.

It also became apparent that this system required children to follow adult direction with very little thinking, an approach that was heavily oriented toward simple obedience. Practitioners realized we had swung too far back into excessive adult control and began to search for alternatives.

**Pendulum to the Left**

In the 1980s, freedom of choice and personal rights became the major social issues. Child advocates argued that the excessive adult control inherent in behavior modification was unacceptable. They suggested that children should be allowed to make their own choices. The theory was that children would learn to be respectful and responsible by experiencing the outcomes of their choices.

Adults were instructed to guide children rather than control them. If children made good choices, adults would reward them in order to encourage more good choices in the future. If children made poor choices, then consequences would be applied to discourage such behavior in the future. This approach was called *behavior management.*

This system was adapted for use in the school environment by adding additional strategies related to dealing with large groups, maintaining on-task behavior and organizing a classroom. This specialized approach was labeled *classroom management,* and it is the system used by most teachers in today's schools. Basic behavior management techniques continue to be used for dealing with individual students or small groups.

Educators adopted management techniques very quickly, partly because this methodology matched a major educational movement that was underway at the same time, a movement called the *discovery* approach to learning. This approach developed when it became clear that in an information-rich world, children would never learn everything they needed to learn if adults simply poured facts into their heads. Instead, it was necessary to teach children how to learn.

School environments were redesigned in an effort to encourage exploration, experimentation, and personal discovery, a change based on the belief that information and concepts learned through personal experience would be remembered longer and understood better. (Although this is generally true, it has been amply demonstrated that direct instruction is also extremely important. Good teachers blend their approaches to accommodate different learning styles.)

Notice the overlap between the discovery approach to learning and behavior management, which is also designed on the premise that children should explore their own world, make their own choices, and discover concepts for themselves. They are expected to learn the value of responsible, respectful behavior by experiencing the outcomes of their actions.

*In effect, we are literally using the discovery approach to discipline.* It isn't working very well. Many people are now expressing concerns about the impact of this approach. They have found that these techniques often fail to produce children who are respectful and responsible. Instead, children tend to become selfish and manipulative. Given freedom of choice, they engage in behaviors that are unacceptable to adults. They underachieve in school, display defiant and uncooperative behaviors, and undertake high-risk activities. They believe it is all about "doing their own thing."

## Here We Go Again

Once again, many people are suggesting that we have gone too far and have lost the healthy balance between adult control and child independence. Given the history of discipline, this would not be a surprise. We can also anticipate that, sooner or later, the pendulum will begin to swing back in the other direction. Already, there are frequent calls for the return of the strap. The only way we can avoid this kind of reverse reaction is to have a clear understanding of what went wrong. Behavior management was supposed to be the solution, but appears to have created as many problems as it solved. How did we lose the healthy balance and get so far off track? What went wrong?

CHAPTER
THREE

Too Much of a Good Thing

# Too Much of a Good Thing

*Choices are important, and children should certainly
be allowed to make the ones that are theirs to make.
It is the only way they can develop a sense of independence.
But, why do we always go too far?*

Children are now surrounded by choices, even the ones they are not yet ready to make. We have essentially entered a new age of permissiveness. Instead of exerting a reasonable level of control over children, many adults simply allow them to "do their own thing."

At home, children are allowed to decide for themselves what clothes to wear, how to do their hair, what to eat and when to go to bed. Their bedrooms are out-of-bounds to adults. Body piercing and tattoos are considered personal issues. In many families, it has reached the point where parents have to bargain with their children just to get a little cooperation.

The school environment is, in many cases, much the same. Lining up is passé. Clothing is a personal statement, and dress codes may be considered an infringement of individual rights. "Punk" talk and actions are accepted as typical adolescent behavior.

And if you ever needed proof that we are back into permissiveness, just consider this: thousands of parents and teachers have accepted the advice that adults should not be saying no to children. Instead, everything should be worded positively. Supposedly, rules such as "No fighting" lower the self-esteem of children and should be changed to "Keep your hands to yourself" or "No body contact."

Get serious! Children need to know their limits, both at home and at school. Using the word *no* is one way to express such limits, particularly the ones that are restrictions on behavior. You would be very hard pressed to find a child who is incapable of learning this concept. Moreover, if adults decline to say no to children, then children grow up without the ability to say no to themselves. That ability is one of the most important parts of self-discipline and self-restraint, and remember—*they learn it from us.*

## No Limits

This permissive approach to discipline constitutes one of the major problems with management strategies since it does not provide effective limits for children. Instead, it often substitutes choices for limits. This problem occurs because one of the most commonly used management strategies involves warning children about the possible outcomes of their behavior, information that is considered crucial to the development of independent thinking.

Hence, instead of saying, "No fighting," a teacher is much more likely to say, "If you fight, you will go to the principal's office." Listen to yourself for a while, and listen to the people around you. You will be amazed at the number of people who talk to children in a litany of "If ... then ..." statements: "If you hand in your work like this, you will get a failing grade." "If you interrupt one more time, you will have a detention." These are choices, not limits!

Saying, "If you fight, you will go to the principal's office" does not disallow fighting at school. It provides a choice. It says, "If you are willing to go to the principal's office, then fighting is one of the choices you get to make at this school to solve your problems." "If you hand in your work like this, you will get a failing grade" actually says, "If you don't mind getting a failing grade, then you have my permission to turn in your work like this."

Don't believe it? Think about sports for a minute. In football, the rules warn that rough play results in a fifteen-yard penalty. Does this mean there is no rough play in football? Obviously not. In hockey, the rules provide a two-minute penalty for tripping. Does this mean there is no tripping in hockey? No. These rules do not prohibit infractions; they merely inform players about the consequences of making poor choices.

Thus the essence of behavior management is choice. Behavior management allows children to choose their behavior solely on the basis of their willingness to live with the consequences. There are several serious problems with this entire concept.

### Just Part of the Game

First, many children view consequences as being "part of the game," a perception that is identical to the way various sports are played. Basketball is a perfect example of this concept because the act of fouling your opponent is part of the strategy, particularly toward the end of a game. Whenever children think something is a game, many of them (especially boys) feel challenged to win. To do so, one of the skills they learn is to adopt an "I don't care" attitude. This gives them immunity to consequences and empowers them by allowing them to ignore one of our most powerful tools.

> **Think penalties are negative?**
>
> Think again! In hockey, taking a two minute tripping penalty to stop a breakaway is called "taking a *good penalty.*"
>
> Penalties and consequences are not always negative. Whether they are good or bad depends on the alternative. Hence, many students think, "If I hit him, I'll be sent to the principal's office. Hmmm. OK, it's worth it."—*POW!*

When students constantly display an "I don't care" attitude, it drives teachers crazy. Not only is it annoying and confrontational, but it also leaves adults feeling like they are losing control. The natural response is to try to convince the students that they really do care. We coax and cajole, explain, discuss, and negotiate. The next step is usually to offer additional rewards—"If you complete your assignment, you can work on the computer"—bargaining with students to get their cooperation and compliance. Additional consequences may also be threatened.

Incredibly, we continue down this path even with students who are so difficult that they are enrolled in special behavioral programs. With these students, we offer major rewards, trying desperately to convince them that following teacher directions is worthwhile. Think about this: Here are students who are already selfish and self-centered. Instead of changing their values, we reinforce them, confirming for these students that their distorted and selfish view of the world is accurate.

Many people support the use of these techniques and believe they work. They certainly do work—for a while. The techniques work because they match the students' value systems, encouraging students to buy into the system long enough to get some of the rewards. Once the novelty wears off, however, the students return to their old behaviors. There is usually no long-term improvement. In fact, these systems essentially amount to playing a game with students, a game called "out-manipulate the manipulator."

There are great ways to use rewards in a classroom. Bribing students to behave well is not one of them. In chapter 8, we will look at more appropriate ways to support positive student behavior in a way that maintains the values of the learning community.

**Is Anyone Watching?**

The second problem is that students learn to win this game by constantly scanning for supervision and immediately taking advantage of low-supervision situations—when the teacher's back is turned, the teacher is working with a group, or the teacher is late getting outside to supervise the playground. In each case, students see these situations as opportunities when they can try to get away with breaking the rules.

Along with this kind of sneakiness go other sneaky behaviors. Students learn to deny their involvement in an incident, challenging teachers to prove any accusations. They learn to blame their behaviors on other students, and they learn to play the role of the victim. "Everyone picks on me. You never believe me. Life is unfair."

**Reversal of Fortune**

The third problem is one that results in many confrontations between adults and children. It develops because behavior management techniques are fairly simplistic and "gamy." Because they involve a great deal of bargaining and negotiating, they lack any sense of adult authority. As a result, many children learn the system and reverse it, using exactly the same techniques to control adult behavior. At home, they can give their parents such a hard time over a simple request to do a chore that the parents will decide that next time, it would be easier to do it themselves. Understand what is taking place. The child is using a consequence to discourage the parents from making that choice again in the future. In effect, the child is disciplining the parents, using exactly the same management techniques the parents were taught to use. It happens all the time. In schools, students can create so many problems in classrooms that teachers are pleased just to have them sitting quietly. It does not matter if they do not accomplish anything. At least they are quiet, and the other students can get their work done.

## Backing Off

When children use these techniques, adults back off. Concerned about how the children will respond, they resist putting demands on children. "But what will I do if he refuses?" "What if he gets all upset and starts to throw things?"

Adults also back off from any active intervention, instead becoming observers and reporters of child misbehaviors. They stand and watch children misbehave, and then report it to somebody else. We have teachers who report student misconduct to school administrators and homeroom teachers. Parents report incidents to their spouses. Worst of all, we have teachers who constantly report misconduct to parents, hoping the parents can do something about their child's conduct even though the incidents occurred outside of parental jurisdiction and supervision. We will discuss better strategies later in the book.

## Nothing Left to Lose

Now, let's take another look at the issue of caring. We already looked at the issue of children who learn to use an "I don't care" attitude as a manipulative device in an attempt to get their own way. It is also important to recognize that many children genuinely do not care about consequences. These are the children who come from difficult home situations. Perhaps they are abused or neglected. Maybe they are dealing with a loss due to divorce or a death in the family.

These children are emotionally numb. They experience so much pain in their everyday lives that their attitude is that any consequences given out by teachers mean nothing. They simply do not care. Consequences not only will not teach them anything, they add to the load. Similarly with rewards, they will accept them if they are offered. On the other hand, if the rewards are taken away, that's OK too. It doesn't matter.

The fact is, consequences only work with children who care about consequences.

**Reflection Is Not Easy**

Finally, let's understand the effect of behavior management on children with learning and attentional difficulties. Learning from consequences requires reflection. It requires children to consider the outcomes of their actions and choices. They must recall what happened to them when they were in certain situations and use that knowledge to change their behavior the next time they find themselves in a similar situation.

This method automatically leaves behind all of the children who are considered impulsive, including those who are severe enough to be diagnosed with Attention Deficit Disorder (ADD). By definition, impulsive children act before they think. If they were able to do all this reflection and use it to govern their own behavior, they would not have been labeled as impulsive and having ADD in the first place. Applying thinking to social problem-solving situations is their handicap. It is precisely the skill they do not have (and may never completely develop). Is it any wonder that impulsive children are struggling in our schools these days?

For an ADD child, a think-for-yourself world is a dangerous world. The moment the child's brain goes into gear, impulsivity rules. Mistakes are inevitable along with the punishment that invariably follows. ADD children need structure, supervision, and adult direction. A substantial portion of each day must be governed by routines that limit the need for them to think about choices and make decisions. For them, an unstructured day is a recipe for disaster.

The same is true for children with learning disabilities (LD). They cannot handle the abstract reasoning demanded by behavior management techniques. They do not have the ability to perceive the impact of their choices on other people or the ability to anticipate how others will respond. They need direct instruction, not just consequences. The only way LD and ADD children learn to be responsible and cooperative is when they are taught to be responsible and cooperative.

Now that you understand the impact and limitations
of relying on behavior management,
let's look at a more balanced approach.

CHAPTER
FOUR

# Renewing Our Sense of Discipline

# Renewing Our Sense
# of Discipline

There is a lot more to discipline
than simply encouraging children to make good choices.
*Discipline is about* preparing *children for all the choices*
*they will be making and ensuring that they are ready to handle them.*

Management approaches do not prepare children in this way. With management, children are allowed to make their own choices as long as they are willing to accept the consequences for their mistakes. For instance, many parents allow their children to stay up late on school nights, with a warning that if they fall asleep in school the next day, they have no one to blame but themselves. The parents think this is some sort of natural and logical consequence. In reality, it is just children being allowed to make choices they are not ready to make. Children do not consider the effects of sleep deprivation on learning, or the potential impact of such behavior on their long-term educational success. They are too busy satisfying their immediate needs. Adults do understand these issues and are supposed to make the call.

To ensure we are clear on this concept of readiness, let's take a look at a detailed example. These days, almost all parents allow their children to try to get their driver's licenses when they turn sixteen (in most jurisdictions). After all, they are old enough and they have their rights, which is what management is all about. With "real" discipline, parents require their children to be sixteen and ready to go for their licenses. To be ready, they must first demonstrate respect for the rights and needs of others, a sense of responsibility regarding important tasks, and the ability to handle minor frustrations without overreacting. Until these behaviors are demonstrated, they may be old enough to drive, but they are not ready to drive.

Unfortunately, we have moved so far away from this concept that even students who attend special behavioral programs will likely be allowed to get their driver's licenses when they turn sixteen, despite the obvious fact that there is absolutely no way they will be ready to handle the task responsibly.

Children need better discipline than this. Let's look at the components of "real" discipline.

### The First of the Triplets: Rules, Limits, and Authority

Think of discipline as having three parts, each of which requires a different set of strategies.

The first deals with rules, limits, and authority, the structural components of our communities. For communities to function effectively and provide reasonable assurance of safety and security, there must be a clear structure that governs the behavior of community members. People must learn how to work within this structure. They must learn to comply with rules and limits and do what they are told to do by people in a legitimate position of authority. Hence, they learn to obey rules for driving, to respect the property of others, and to stop when police officers instruct them to do so. *This is the "training" part of discipline.*

It is supposed to start when children are very young. In the first year of life, the world revolves around them and their needs. They learn to use crying as a means of summoning adults and having their needs met. Around the age of two, children begin to walk and they experience discipline for the first time as their parents establish limits regarding where they may go and what they may touch. It is at this point that training begins. Parents begin to train their children to obey rules and limits and comply with parental instructions.

Children usually resist this change, a time period we refer to as the "terrible twos." If the parents stick with the training and remain consistent, then dramatic changes take place. By the time their children are four or five years of age, their children know most of the basic structural rules for dealing with school. They know that they will not get their own way all the time, temper tantrums will not work, a big person will be in charge, and they have to do what they are told to do.

Today's discipline does not include the training component. Parents have been advised to use behavior management techniques, even with young children. As a result, many parents negotiate and bargain with their youngsters. They explain parental decisions, and allow their children to make many of their own decisions. Unfortunately, these children are then untrained and often continue to show their two- to four-year-old behaviors right up into adolescence. If they do not get their own way, they have tantrums, lash out, blame others, and refuse to obey instructions.

The next time you are dealing with a difficult child, try looking at the child's behaviors from a developmental point of view. There is a very good chance the behaviors will be typical of very young children.

## The Second Triplet: Skills, Attitudes, and Knowledge

In addition to learning about structure, children must also learn the skills, attitudes, and knowledge associated with being responsible and cooperative. They must learn to be courteous, to work and play with others, to resolve conflicts, and to set personal goals. They must learn how to organize tasks and manage time. They also need to learn the important skill of self-discipline so they will be ready for independence. After all, adults will not always be with them to govern their choices and decisions. They have to learn how to do it by themselves. *This is the "teaching" part of discipline.*

These skills are not learned by accident. No child masters the complex skill of responsibility merely by experiencing the outcomes of personal choices, which is what management techniques assume. Instead, these skills must be systematically taught using appropriate teaching techniques. These include direct instruction, practice, correction, and review.

Some schools attempt to provide this instruction through social skills programs. Although these programs have their place, they are intended to supplement, not replace, the teaching that goes on every day with good discipline. The best way to teach behavioral skills is in ordinary, everyday interactions between adults and children, not out of a binder.

In addition, parents and teachers must require children to use these skills in their everyday interactions. There is no benefit to teaching children their courtesy skills if the children are then permitted to behave in a disrespectful manner.

### Last But Not Least

If children are to become responsible adults, they need to be given more freedom as they get older. They need to be given opportunities to make their own choices and learn from personal experience. The role of adults is to provide guidance throughout this process, helping children to identify appropriate choices and ensuring that they take the rights and needs of others into account. *This is the "management" part of discipline.*

You already have a high level of expertise with management techniques. Since they are an important part of discipline, this means you do not have to drop your present strategies. Rather, it is a matter of refining them so they work in conjunction with the other parts of discipline. What you really want to be doing is giving choices to well-trained, well-taught children. With a solid foundation in place, they are likely to make their choices responsibly and with respect for the rights and needs of others.

### Putting It All Together

Here's a quick way of seeing these components together. For effective discipline, you should do the following:

- Train students to comply with rules, limits, and adult directions
- Teach students the skills, attitudes, and knowledge required to be responsible and cooperative
- Manage their independent choices

## Establish a Healthy Balance

These three sets of strategies must be blended together and employed as needed. To understand how this idea works, just think of the methodology employed for teaching children to read. To ensure that all children learn to read, regardless of their learning styles, good teachers blend three approaches. They teach children to break words into their component parts and sound them out, a process called phonics. They also teach children to use the visualization capabilities of the brain that allow children to recognize words simply by looking at them, the "sight" approach. Then, to ensure that words are not just squiggles on a page, teachers give them real-life context by applying them to children's experiences, an approach known as "language experience" or "whole language." All three approaches must be used or a significant number of students would be left behind, a problem that was demonstrated in dramatic fashion when the whole language approach became trendy and was used exclusively by a significant number of teachers.

Discipline is exactly the same. All three approaches must be utilized or a significant number of students would be left behind (which is exactly what is happening in today's schools where management approaches have dominated).

It is also important for a healthy balance to be established in the use of these strategies. When children are young, the training and teaching techniques should be emphasized. This is the time for developing a solid foundation in a child's life, preparing them for greater independence in the future. As children get older, training should be decreased and more emphasis should be placed on choices. We want children to have more and more choices as they grow older so they are ready for independence. However, always remember that you want to be giving choices to well-trained, well-taught children. They are the only children who handle their choices responsibly and with respect for the rights and needs of others.

# CHAPTER FIVE

# Believe It or Not

# Believe It or Not

When teachers are concerned about discipline, they invariably go on a search for new strategies. Fortunately, there is no shortage of resources to support this search. There are books that list strategies for almost every conceivable discipline issue. Some of them are like cookbooks in which you look up the specific behavior and turn to the "recipe" for dealing with it. There are also many workshops and seminars available that focus on discipline and behavioral interventions.

However, if you really want great discipline, you must understand that strategies are only half of the puzzle. Discipline is also a set of beliefs, and you must be willing to look at your beliefs if you want to improve your effectiveness in this area. *The outcome of your strategies is determined as much by your beliefs as by the strategies themselves.*

Thus two teachers can use the same strategy but end up with totally different results. For example, consider a situation in which a student is having serious difficulty concentrating with thirty other students in close proximity to him. One possible solution for this problem would be to create a quiet work area by placing a study carrel at the back of the classroom and teaching the student to use it whenever necessary.

One teacher will implement the strategy by approaching the student during class and saying, "Bill, I notice you're not getting your work done. This would be an excellent time for you to go back to the study carrel. Get your work done there and show it to me when you're finished." This is exactly how the strategy was meant to be used.

However, another teacher will approach the student and say, "Bill, I notice you're not getting your work done. If you don't settle down right now, you will have to go and work in the study carrel, understand?"

Same strategy, two totally different ways of using it—one is positive and one is negative. The first teacher perceives discipline as a way of teaching children to behave appropriately. Hence, the student is sent to an alternate location to accomplish his work. The second teacher perceives discipline as something to threaten students with if they do not do as they are told. In this case, a perfectly good study skill (choosing a quiet location to do your work) is used as a threat.

Almost every strategy is affected in this way:
- Time-outs can be used to help children or to reject them.
- The word no can be positive limit-setting or negative scolding.
- Likewise, detentions, lost privileges, and even rewards are altered by the beliefs of the person using them.

**Punishment or Guidance?**

The deciding factor is how people perceive discipline itself. There are people who believe that discipline is synonymous with punishment and consequences. When they talk about disciplining children, they are thinking about time-outs and lost privileges.

Other people believe that discipline is about guiding children. When they talk about discipline, they are thinking about limit setting and the teaching of essential skills. Look discipline up in the dictionary, and you will mostly be reading about these concepts. The first five or six definitions are almost invariably about teaching and training children to be the kind of children you want them to be. Punishment is noted, of course, because it is part of discipline, but it is not the dominant theme.

**What Do You Believe?**

What is your first thought when you hear that a student is being sent to the office for discipline? Do you instantly think the student is in trouble? Or do you assume that the principal will be resolving a problem with the student but you don't know how? There could indeed be some penalties assessed, but the resolution could just as easily entail discussion, compensation, or any number of other possibilities.

If you immediately think that the student would be punished, then perhaps it is time to take a serious look at your beliefs regarding discipline. The effectiveness of your strategies will be greatly enhanced if you adopt a positive view. Take a moment to consider the following inscription that is on the cornerstone of Assumption High School in Windsor, Ontario: *Please teach us goodness, discipline, and knowledge.* It is impossible to read this inscription and still believe that discipline is synonymous with punishment.

## Prevention First

Since behavior management relies on the use of rewards and consequences, it is inherently reactive. It is a system that allows children to make their choices and then governs how adults respond to those choices.

In the last chapter, however, we established the concept that effective discipline has three essential components, not just one. In addition to behavior management, there are also the training and teaching components. Both of these are proactive. Since training and teaching are the foundation components of discipline, discipline itself is mostly proactive. It is about preventing incidents, not responding to them. Hence, effective teachers believe that *discipline is not what you do when children misbehave; it is what you do so they will not.*

Thus, you should not be asking, "What should I do if he hits another student?" You should ask, "What should I do so he won't hit another student?" It is a completely different question and has a completely different answer.

Similarly, do not ask, "What should I do when students interrupt?" Ask, "What should I do so students won't interrupt?" Plan for how students will behave well, instead of planning how you will respond if they behave poorly.

**Needs Versus Deserves**

The constant focus on consequences has led many people to believe that discipline is all about giving kids what they deserve. You will frequently hear comments such as, "He doesn't deserve to go on the field trip," and "He doesn't deserve any time on the computer." Once again, this is not the belief system that is associated with positive discipline. *Discipline is about giving children what they need, not what they deserve.*

A student may not deserve to go on a field trip. However, field trips are part of the curriculum. They are used to teach students that lessons taught in the classroom apply to the outside world. All students need to learn this lesson. The fact that it is one of the most exciting parts of the curriculum does not mean it should be taken away. (There are certainly situations in which students should not go on trips because of safety concerns, but safety is a different issue.) Similarly, students need to be on the computers to learn skills for the modern world. Their computer use has nothing to do with whether or not they deserve to be on the computers.

This is not to say that consequences have no place in the classroom. But you should be very careful how you teach them about consequences. Students clearly have to learn what happens when they behave a certain way. They also need to learn that no means no. With the computer, for instance, it would certainly be reasonable to deny a student access to an extra game that the teacher provided as a motivational tool. This is not something the child needs. Similarly, a student could be denied extra privileges.

**From Whose Experience?**

Finally, it was noted earlier that behavior management is essentially the discovery approach to discipline. It is designed around the concept that children learn best from their own experience. It would be wise to remember this old saying: *It's the unlucky who learn from experience; the lucky learn from the experience of others.*

Our job is to teach children the important lessons about life so they will not have to learn them the hard way. As adults, we already know the following:

- How easily one can get hooked on drugs
- What happens when children play with guns
- That smoking is addictive, not cool
- That a breakup during adolescence is not the end of the world
- That thinner does not mean prettier

Our children should not have to learn these lessons for themselves. They should learn them from us. We are supposed to be protecting our children from life's painful experiences, not using these experiences as teaching tools. These are only a few of the beliefs that you will be asked to examine as you go through this book. We must still look at issues ranging from teamwork to values, so keep an open mind.

**Think Positively**

Your beliefs about discipline are very important. To be truly effective, however, you must also believe in your abilities and the likelihood of success. A positive attitude is crucial.

If you believe children will obey your commands, they will. Your confidence will come across in your voice and in your overall demeanor. This assertiveness will likely elicit a quick, appropriate response from students.

On the other hand, if you are uncertain about your ability to take charge and worried that students may defy you, then they will likely fulfill this expectation as well.

# Fundamentals
## Taking a Closer Look at
## Training, Teaching, and Managing

CHAPTER SIX

# Training Positive Behavior

# Training Positive Behavior

To understand how training techniques work, start by answering this question. When you are driving your car and the traffic light ahead of you turns red, why do you stop? Your initial response would probably be that you stop for safety reasons. Safety is certainly an overriding concern but, if you are well trained, it is not why you stop. This fact becomes obvious when you realize that you would also stop for the red light at three o'clock in the morning in the middle of nowhere with no cars around you for as far as you can see. Then, maybe you think you stop in order to avoid the possible consequence of receiving a traffic ticket. Not likely, because at three o'clock in the morning in the middle of nowhere, the police are not likely to be waiting there just for you. The real reason you stop is much simpler. Assuming you are a well-trained driver, you stop because you always stop. It is a habit.

This response is totally different from the one that behavior management techniques generate. Since behavior management techniques focus on choices, they generate *thinking responses*. You are expected to "mull over" the possibilities. Habits, on the other hand, are nonthinking responses. They come from a different part of the brain. Whereas thinking responses come from the cerebral cortex where cognitive thinking takes place, nonthinking responses are believed to come from part of the limbic system where habits and routines are stored.

## Do You Want Routines or Events?

When students are well trained, they comply with rules and directions for the same reason you do—because they always comply. It is a habit.

Have you seen classrooms where the students enter quickly and quietly, and then get to work immediately? Have you watched with admiration as students stop talking immediately and listen when the teacher asks for their attention? Have you watched teachers who can switch from one subject to another and have the students back on task in about a minute? In each case, order is accomplished by training the students to have good habits and then embedding the habits in routines in order to sustain them. Unfortunately, most teachers are presently bringing these behaviors out of the thinking part of the brain, because they have been taught to do it that way. By doing so, they do not get habits and routines; they get events!

There is a big difference between these two types of responses. Consider the above example in which the teacher switches the class from one subject to another. If this were done as a thinking response, the teacher would indicate that it is time to change from one subject to another, and right away the students would begin to socialize. It would probably be five minutes before the next lesson started and they were back on task. Similarly, entry routines can easily become seven minutes instead of three. Initially, these differences may not sound particularly significant. However, research has found that there are approximately thirty transitions every day in an average elementary school classroom. If four minutes are wasted on every transition, the effect is staggering: *30 x 4 minutes = 2 hours of wasted time.* Reversing this effect by establishing efficient routines would be the equivalent of adding an extra term onto the school year! Hence, the obvious question is, how do you create good habits and routines?

### Sweat the Small Stuff

Ironically, if you want to have well-trained students, you must do the exact opposite of one of the most common recommendations made by experts in behavior management. This recommendation came about after teachers found out that management techniques are very time-consuming. All the explaining and negotiating, the provision of rewards, and the supervision of consequences can use up a great deal of every day. When teachers complained about this problem, they were advised to make the system more practical by overlooking small behaviors. "Pick your battles," they said. "Don't sweat the small stuff." "If it isn't life threatening or morally threatening, don't worry about it."

Be very cautious about following this advice. The concept of ignoring behavior was developed in all of those experiments done with rats in Skinner boxes. Rats operate on a pure stimulus-response system. With this type of functioning, any behavior that is not reinforced tends to diminish. However, it does not work the same way with people. People have the ability to reason. They interpret the world around them. Hence, if you walk by children who are doing something wrong and you say nothing and do nothing, the children interpret your actions as permission and escalate the behavior. Always remember, *behavior you ignore is behavior you permit.*

In reality, you can ignore one type of misbehavior, an attention-seeking misbehavior, but it is the only type that responds positively to being ignored. But, if you ignore defiance, aggression, and bullying, they will escalate so quickly that you will have serious difficulty regaining control.

The real warning you should have received about your strategies for dealing with small behaviors is that you should not punish every little thing that kids do wrong, because you do not want to be an ogre or create a negative environment. (Watch out for the tendency to unwittingly use the most common punishment—scolding.) But just because you do not punish the small stuff, it does not mean you overlook it.

If you want to create good habits and routines, you are required to take charge of the small behaviors, correct them, and insist that they be done properly often enough for them to become habitual. You must do so with small behaviors because only small behaviors will go to the nonthinking part of the brain. Big behaviors usually do not happen frequently enough to become habitual. Also, just because of their size, big behaviors tend to vary somewhat each time, and this variance takes them to the thinking part of the brain. Hence, to train various procedures, you must break the procedures into small components and ensure that they are done sequentially. For instance, there could be ten steps in a basic entry routine. Identify each one within the sequence and have the students do it before moving on to the next one. "First, line up at the door." "Next,..."

The training techniques are used for any behaviors where you want them to be smooth, repetitious, and automatic. Fire drills are an excellent example. Also, consider training various procedures such as handing work in, taking specific materials out of desks, moving from one area to another, and so on. It is possible to quickly generate a lengthy list of procedures that are best dealt with in this way.

### Compliance—The Most Important Routine

Of all the behaviors you should teach, the most important is compliance. Well-trained students do what their teacher tells them to do merely because they always do what their teacher tells them to do: it is just a habit. It is the same compliant response that you have when stopping at red lights.

Let's deal immediately with the concern that many people raise in regard to this concept. They believe this methodology would make students into robots and take us back to the days when students were supposed to be passive, with no opinions of their own, no freedom, and no rights.

Fortunately, there is no need to worry, because that is not what is being recommended. The key is to remember that real discipline has a healthy balance to it. If compliance training were the only technique recommended in this book, then the concern would be totally justified. People should also be concerned about behavior management that goes to the other extreme and completely ignores the value of such training. Neither extreme is desirable.

### Compliance Has Its Time and Place

Compliance training is appropriate for ordinary actions and procedures in which cognitive responses would waste time and create undesirable disruption. Entry and exit procedures are a good example.

They should also be used to govern student responses to "low-level" teacher directions. For example, when you instruct a student to take out a particular book, you do not want a cognitive response—"Why should I? I do not want to get that book right now. Why can't I finish this book first?" When you instruct a student to pick up a pencil that is lying on the floor, you do not want to hear, "It's not my pencil. I didn't drop it. Why do I have to pick it up?"

With ordinary actions such as these, you want the students to comply without getting their brains in gear over it. Similarly, you want an automatic response when you instruct a student to stop, to come and talk to you, or to open a book and get to work.

To do compliance training, you must get compliance on many small directions in order to set the foundation for compliance on bigger items. For example, teacher-directed warm-up exercises are a good way to start physical education periods because the multiple directions create a foundation for compliance during the other activities. A simple warm-up exercise may require students to comply with as many as one hundred teacher directions.

Unless you build a strong foundation, you will likely be dealing with a high level of disruptive and defiant behavior. For instance, when a student will not open his book and get to work at the beginning of first period, take a good look at the few minutes leading up to this incident. Almost invariably, the student was allowed to do the following, and nobody stopped him and sent him back to do it right:

- Enter the classroom speaking in his outside voice
- Bump into other students on his way in
- Throw his jacket somewhere instead of hanging it up
- Slide his backpack across the floor
- Wander around the room instead of doing bell work (routine activities that are done to prepare for class)
- Lie across his desk during opening exercises
- Talk during announcements

You must take care of the small behaviors, not to be picky, but to set a foundation for compliance on big behaviors.

**Just Do It**

There is another key to effective training in addition to the need to govern small behaviors. *Training is non-conversational.* Training instills behaviors in the nonthinking part of the brain. The moment you begin to discuss, explain, or converse, you are in the thinking part of the brain. Hence, training utilizes short command statements such as, "Line up at the door," "Hang up your jackets," and "Stand up straight." The statements are short and to the point. They are also said with authority. If students ask for an explanation, you can provide it but not during the training. Delay your explanation until the training is complete.

**Think Like a Driving Instructor**

Driver training provides a great example of how these techniques are applied. The instructor gets in the car with you and says, "First, fasten your seat belt." Notice the use of the short command statement. The instructor does not say, "If you don't mind, I would really appreciate it if you would put your seat belt on, okay?" Approaching it in this fashion would immediately start a conversation, and the training would be ineffective. The lesson then proceeds with one short instruction after another. If the student were to start asking a lot of questions, the instructor would respond with, "Concentrate on your driving. We'll talk later." Questions are answered, but not during the training. Also take note that the instructor sits right next to you in the car. This is absolutely essential because training requires direct supervision. *Discipline cannot be done from a distance.*

You must be supervising the students to do the job. Note that this has nothing to do with age. Even if you were fifty years old and learning to drive, the instructor would still sit right next to you in the car. It has to do with what you are trying to accomplish. Therefore, supervision is as important in middle schools and secondary schools as it is at the elementary level! It is applied differently, but it must still be done. A great deal of bullying behavior occurs on the school grounds surrounding secondary schools. There are absolutely no effective techniques for dealing with this behavior if there are no staff members outside supervising the students. *Supervision for adolescents is supposed to be nonintrusive, not nonexistent.*

Adolescents need some room to spread their wings because they are learning about independence. However, they should not be allowed to wander around, doing whatever they want to do. To understand the high-priority nature of this issue, make sure you read the example in the box below.

As we leave this section, consider the following: The next time you hear yourself saying, "Don't even think about it," you will know you are doing the training part of discipline.

## The Right Stuff

R. H. King Academy is a unique secondary school in the Toronto area. Although it is part of the public school system, it is designated as a special "high standards school." Its popularity is such that parents "camp out" overnight just to be able to enroll their children.

The high standards at R. H. King Academy apply not only to academics but to behavior as well. What does it take to accomplish this goal at the secondary level? According to the academy's vice-principal, "The biggest difference between our academy and all the other secondary schools is that we supervise our students. If you were to come here when classes are on rotation, you would find every teacher in the hallways. It's required. And it doesn't matter which teacher deals with a situation; the students will receive the same message because every teacher knows what is expected at this school."

Right on! Now, all we have to do is make every school into a "high standards" school.

CHAPTER SEVEN

# Teaching Responsible Behavior

# Teaching Responsible Behavior

*Well-trained students obey rules.*

*Well-taught students understand why we need rules and why teachers are given the authority to enforce them.*

*They also know the skills and attitudes associated with responsible, respectful conduct.*

As an educator, you already have an extensive knowledge of teaching strategies. You know the processes for skill development, knowledge acquisition, and the development of higher order thinking skills such as analyzing and synthesizing. If you want great students, you must apply these same processes to discipline. Unless students are taught how to behave appropriately, they will not do so. The discovery approach to discipline does not work.

Behavior management and classroom management lack this teaching component, relying instead on the ability of students to learn skills and attitudes from personal experience. Over the years, many professionals have become concerned about the deteriorating level of social skills in students and have implemented social skills programs in an attempt to compensate for this deficiency.

Unfortunately, social skills programs work only if they are integrated with the broader discipline strategies and expectations employed by teachers throughout the school environment, a situation that rarely occurs.

Instead, the programs are usually implemented by one "passionate" individual, and the program ceases when that individual moves on to a different job. It is not truly part of the school program.

## Discipline Is Every Minute of Every Day

"Real" discipline does not rely on the implementation of add-on programs. Instead, it ensures that behavioral skills are learned in the most efficient and effective way—in ordinary, everyday interactions between adults and students. Courtesy, for instance, is not supposed to be taught as lesson fifteen from a program or textbook. It is taught when a teacher hands something to a student but will not let go until the student says "thank you."

Unfortunately, this kind of teaching is not very common these days. We have all been taught to allow students to "be themselves." We are supposed to accept the lack of courtesy from kids as being typical. Besides, you are not supposed to sweat the small stuff, remember?

When you say "good morning" to students, do you insist that they return your greeting? Most teachers do not. They appreciate the students who do respond but ignore the ones who do not. This tendency to overlook teaching opportunities results in countless missed lessons. Instead of complaining that kids are not courteous these days, we need to avail ourselves of these opportunities and teach them to be the kind of students we want them to be.

## Responding to Mistakes

An inherent part of teaching is the continuous correction of student errors. Errors are an important part of the process, and we actually design the curriculum and activities to ensure that a healthy number of them will be made. Too few would indicate that the assignments were not sufficiently challenging. If there were too many, students would be frustrated by their inability to do the work.

Every teacher knows the basic techniques for responding to errors—correct, review, reteach, practice. Now, take a minute and consider what would happen if this process was changed. What if the following techniques were employed?

- Every time a student makes a mistake in mathematics, the student is assigned a two-minute time-out.
- For mistakes in creative writing, the student is given a detention.
- Mistakes on a science quiz result in the loss of a privilege.

Absurd? Obviously, and no teacher would ever consider using these strategies. If any teacher did, students would quickly reach the point of hating school and hating the teacher.

Then explain why we use these techniques in discipline. A student speaks rudely to a teacher and the teacher says, "If you talk that way to me again, you will be sitting in a time-out." First, remember that this is a choice. It actually says, "If you don't mind sitting in a time-out, then being rude to me is one of the things you get to do at this school." Second, what is the purpose of the time-out? Courtesy is a skill that, like mathematics, is learned through direct instruction and positive practice, not punishment. You can give a student time-outs for rudeness ten times every day, and he still will not learn to be courteous. He will learn how to take time-outs. We are supposed to be correcting errors. The teacher's response should be, "We don't speak that way at this school. Now, start over." *Most of the time when we punish children, we actually do not need them to be punished. We need them to behave correctly.*

### "No Way"

This does not mean consequences and punishment do not have a place in discipline. They are important strategies, but rarely the strategy of first choice. Suppose in the previous example that the student, instructed to start over, responded with defiance and said, "No way. You can't make me." First, you should lower your voice, become more serious and more assertive, and repeat your instruction. However, if the student continues to be defiant, then a consequence would be perfectly appropriate. Just remember, when the consequence is over, the student still has to come back and be polite. Discipline is not finished until you get the correct behavior.

### Need Proof

Perhaps you aren't yet convinced that the teaching part of discipline is missing from the management approach employed in today's schools. Here's a challenge. Get a copy of your school's code of conduct. Turn to the section where it lists teacher responses to student misconduct. See if you can find a teaching word in the section. Did you find the word correct? Where's teach, review, instruct, and practice? Chances are, you didn't find them at all. Our present codes of conduct reflect management's reliance on consequences.

If you want to remedy the problem, make sure the first line in this section of your code says, "Correct the student." Then you can add, "Teach the student to behave better tomorrow." Add, "Have the student practice the correct behavior." You might even want to consider putting in words like research, investigate, and so on. We need to start using our best techniques—teaching techniques.

P.S. If your code of conduct does reflect a teaching approach, congratulations! You're ahead of the times.

## Practice Makes Perfect

Practice is an essential component of learning new skills. It is important for learning behavioral skills as well. Courtesy is learned by being courteous over and over again. Unfortunately, behavior management presents repetition as a consequence, something to be avoided if possible.

To overcome this problem, relate practice to sports. Tiger Woods is an extraordinary golfer. Where does he spend his time before and after a round of golf? On the practice tee. He does not do this because he is not good at golf. He practices to stay good and get even better.

It is also why baseball players have batting practice before a game, and right before they go up to bat as well. Plus, if they get in a slump, they take extra batting practice—extra repetitions of the correct behavior. Remember never to threaten a student with practice. If it is needed, assign it. Discipline gives children what they need, not what they deserve.

**Timing Is Everything**

As a teacher, you understand when practice should be done. You have students practice mathematics before a test so they will do well during the test. The physical education teacher has students practice their basketball skills before a game so they will do well during the game.

Trying to practice skills at the same time as they are needed is too stressful. Coaches who try to teach skills during the course of a game get all stressed out. They shout at players and go into a frenzy when things are done incorrectly. During a game, you can correct players but it is not a good time for teaching. The same is true when behavioral skills are being taught. In the middle of a lesson, correct behaviors. If practice is needed, schedule it for a time when the pressure is off. Whenever possible, pre-teach skills. Teach your students how to behave in an assembly when there is not an assembly going on, so they know how to behave when they go to one. Teach your students the classroom procedures when there is no pressure to implement them. Then they will know what to do when you need a procedure followed quickly. Remember, we practice fire drills when there is not a fire, so the students will know what to do if there is one.

*Be a good role model.* Children learn by example, especially for any behavior that involves values. Teachers who are courteous, enthusiastic, patient, and organized are good role models for students. Being such a teacher says, "Watch me. This is how you do it. Now, you do it the same way."

**More Powerful Than Punishment**

When students are running down a hallway, sending them back to walk is far more effective than scolding them or giving a consequence. The following example was first printed in the book *Secrets of Discipline* that preceded this book. The example was so well received that it seemed worthy of being reprinted here. It would be difficult to find a better example of the power of educational techniques.

**Caught Speeding**

If you are not convinced that positive practice is more effective than punishment, consider the following scenario. You are driving to a meeting in another city. Halfway through the two-hour trip, flashing red lights appear in your rearview mirror and you realize that the police are pulling you over for speeding. You wonder how big the fine will be. "Oh, well," you say to yourself. "There's nothing I can do about it now. Hopefully, this won't take too long and I can still make my meeting."

The officer is now standing at your car door. "You were speeding," he states. "Now, you go all the way back home and do your trip over again at the right speed!" Then the officer attaches a monitoring device to your car to ensure that you do exactly what you have been told to do.

If this happened to you, would you slow down on future trips? You bet you would! Right now, the police are limited to handing out speeding tickets. Many people ignore this potential consequence and continue to speed. Busy people may even consider the occasional ticket to be the price they have to pay for getting places on time. And, of course, they quickly learn to watch for supervision, just like children do. They slow down when they see a police car and speed up once they are out of sight. Welcome to the world of behavior management.

**Examine Your Beliefs**

Look at the two statements used earlier:

• "If you talk that way to me again, you will be sitting in a time-out" (behavior management).

   *Management communicates what will happen to you if you make a poor choice.*

• "We don't speak that way at this school. Now, start over" (discipline).

   *Discipline communicates that the only way you will behave is the right way.*

This latter statement is the belief of all great disciplinarians. They consistently convey the message that there is only one way you will behave, so get used to it.

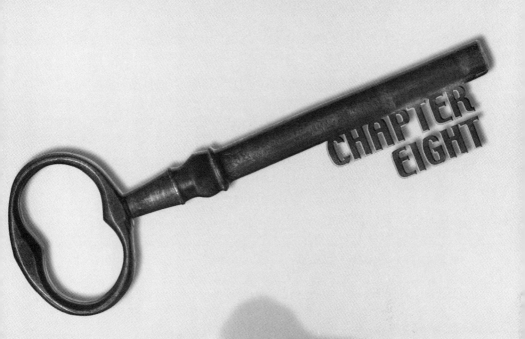

CHAPTER
EIGHT

# Managing Independent Behavior

# Managing Independent Behavior

You are already aware of the basic management approaches:

- Provide students with choices
- Encourage good choices through the use of rewards and guidance
- Discourage poor choices through the use of consequences and warnings about potential undesirable outcomes
- Allow students to learn by experiencing the outcomes of their choices

*When management strategies are utilized within an overall discipline approach, these strategies are employed in a different fashion. Give them choices when they are ready.* Rather than simply allowing students to decide everything for themselves, determine their readiness to handle the choices:

- Do they have the skills and attitudes necessary to make a responsible, independent decision?
- Do they understand the long-term implications of their decision?
- Do they care about the outcome and its impact on other people?

Is this a choice that can be transferred to students or is it intended to be an adult responsibility?

For instance, many students do not care about their marks. Until they do, they are not ready to make decisions about the quality of their work. The teacher decides when the work is ready to be submitted. Some choices are not for students to make, even if they are willing to live with the consequences. Among these are underachievement and violence.

Do not feel obligated to provide the same choice to everyone because of a misguided sense of fairness. If some students are ready and others are not, make the call. To demonstrate fairness, all you have to do is guarantee that the other students will also be allowed to make this choice as soon as they are ready to do so.

*Use rewards to support discipline, not to replace discipline.* Avoid using rewards as a means of getting students to behave. Using rewards in this way leads to bargaining and negotiating. In addition, it breeds selfishness in the students and creates a different value system in which students behave in order to get something. These students frequently make comments such as, "Why should I? What do I get? What's in it for me?"

With discipline, you are supposed to teach students to behave well and train them to follow rules. Initially, you must support your instruction with your authority, not with rewards. When they do behave appropriately, you can then provide rewards to reinforce their actions.

Whenever possible, use "shared" rewards. Rather than giving a student some popcorn as a reward, have the student select several other students who will also receive the reward. Sometimes, provide the reward to the entire class. Not only does a shared award discourage selfishness, but it also serves to raise the social status of the student who earned the reward. This type of reward has far greater benefits in the long run than could be accomplished by providing the popcorn as an individual reward.

Sometimes, shared rewards are as simple as setting up a rule that says, "If you get a sticker from me, you must also take one for someone else." This simple act supports the goal of helping students to think about others.

Make absolutely certain that your use of rewards matches the values that you are trying to instill in your students.

> *Bargaining, bribing, and threatening*
> *teach students to do what is advantageous.*
> *Discipline teaches them to do what is right.*

*Apply consequences with purpose.* Consequences should not reflect adult frustration, rejection, or revenge. When you are disciplining effectively, even your consequences should carry a purposeful, and therefore positive, message. With discipline, consequences are always used to accomplish something. With training approaches, the purpose is to convey the messages, "No means No" and "Don't even think about it!" These messages are important for reinforcing the sense of threshold because there are some behaviors that are not supposed to cross that barrier under any circumstance.

The teaching part of discipline employs review and practice as natural consequences. When errors are made, skills need additional work. Students need to practice more or learn more in order to behave appropriately. In the management part of discipline, consequences are used to discourage students from making poor choices.

**Keep Your Consequences Flexible**

Many codes of conduct developed for schools "lock in" specific consequences for particular actions, a serious error that is usually based on a mistaken notion about what it means to be consistent. Consistency is primarily an issue of expectations. You need to consistently expect courtesy, for instance. Doing so allows you to correct misbehavior whenever you see it.

You also want to be consistent with your messages. Hence, anytime a student "puts down" another student, you want to give a clear "No" message. How you do this, however, can vary, and this is the reason you do not want to lock in your consequences. There are students who will learn "No" from "La Look" (We all know the withering look that teachers learn to use so well). Other students may need a time-out. Some might need to lose a privilege, and a few might need to be suspended. Everyone should get the message, but they do not all get it the same way. How unfortunate it would be if a student who only needed a time-out were suspended simply because the school's code of conduct only provided one option.

You must also be willing to vary your consequences according to a child's level of competence, the general rule being that you do not punish incompetence. If a boy in eighth grade kisses a girl against her will, it is misconduct. If a boy in kindergarten does likewise, it is not misconduct. The boy in kindergarten is incompetent. There is no way he understands issues like sexual harassment. He needs to be taught, not punished. As professional educators, we are supposed to know that teaching is the proper response to incompetence.

The above example did, in fact occur, and the kindergarten child was suspended for his actions, as per the dictates of the code of conduct. Another much publicized episode involved a first-grade student being suspended for bringing his teacher a bottle of wine as a Christmas present, thereby violating the school's restrictions regarding alcohol on school grounds. The child had no idea he was violating anything! Do not throw your professional judgment out the window.

There is also the issue of intent. You should vary your consequences in accordance with the deliberateness of a student's act. There is a big difference between a student spontaneously emitting a swear word in response to frustration and another student deliberately directing a swear word at someone else. The second case is violent; the first is not. You will often need to punish deliberate misconduct. You rarely need to do so for spontaneous acts.

### Keep Learning in Mind

Consequences do not have to be punitive. In addition to the typical consequences, consider the following advanced options.

**Compensation:** Have the student do something positive to make up for doing something negative. Positive activities could include making his victim feel better, making the school look better, organizing an activity for others, and so on.

**Letter writing:** Have a misbehaving student write a letter to the victim(s) of his actions. Insist that any apologies be sincere. Have the student include a commitment regarding future actions, provided that the commitment is genuine.

**Improvement Plans:** Have a student create a plan for how he will handle a situation better in the future. Keep the plan and follow up with it at a specified interval. Mark the follow-up date on a calendar. If the plan has been implemented successfully, celebrate. If not, then it needs to be refined.

**Research:** Have a student research the issue that is at the forefront of his behavioral difficulties. Include interviews with other students and adults. It may also be possible to have the student contact organizations, social services, or government agencies in order to get materials that would be useful to the school as a whole. These materials could be distributed or become part of the student's work.

**Teach lessons to younger children:** Have a student write and illustrate a book that can then be read to students in lower grades. The story should indicate what the student has learned about his specific issue.

These techniques help students behave better in the future, which is the central focus of behavioral interventions. Remember never to threaten students with learning. Do not say, "If you do that again, you're going to have to do research and write a book."

### Keep Guidance Focused

Guidance is important. It helps students identify critical factors involved in their decisions, helps them weigh the pros and cons, and ensures that they take their responsibilities into account along with the rights and needs of others. However, several serious problems may occur if guidance is not provided in a way that fits with the overall discipline process.

As with consequences, ensure that guidance is purposeful. There is a big difference between guiding a student's decision making and bargaining in an attempt to get cooperation. Unfortunately, far too many people go down this road. They allow a student to make a choice that he was not ready to make. Then, they use their guidance as a way of coaxing him into making the desired decision. We all know of situations in which an adult has counseled a student for over an hour just to get him to do a ten-minute task. When coaxing does not work, then the bargaining and negotiating begin. Don't go there. If students are not ready to make certain choices, then it is up to adults to make the decisions.

Another problem that frequently occurs during guidance sessions is that adults may inadvertently create excuses for student misconduct. The adult inquires, "Why did you hit Joey?" and Bill responds, "I was angry." Many adults accept this rationale and immediately take it further by asking,

"And what made you angry?" This process creates a direct link between anger and aggression in the student's mind and allows him to rationalize his actions. In fact, there are millions of angry people in the world who do not hit anybody. Always deal with these issues separately. First, discuss the aggression. Then, you may choose to discuss the anger, but do not link the two issues together. Watch out for links with home problems, the behavior of other students, and school issues such as marks.

Finally, if guidance is done in school, make sure it stays focused on school. The purpose of school-based guidance is not to discuss a divorce that is happening in a student's home life; it is to discuss how the student can cope with school when a divorce is happening at home. This educational focus helps the student by maintaining the barrier between home and school, and this barrier is especially important when problems are occurring. When adults have problems in their home environment, they usually do not want to discuss the issues at all when they get to work. It is important to have a safe place, and students need one as well. Also remember that students should receive counseling when they need it, not when an adult's schedule determines it will occur. Frequently, people deal with difficult issues in their lives by putting the issues "on the back burner" for a while. Students often need to do likewise.

### On to Classroom Management

Classroom management is a subset of behavior management. It is a valuable set of strategies as long as the techniques are used in conjunction with great training and great teaching. Let's take a look some useful classroom management strategies.

# CHAPTER NINE

# Effective Classroom Management

# Effective Classroom Management

One of the most consistent findings in all of the studies of effective schools is that learning must be the highest priority. Hence, every teacher should have a repertoire of techniques for keeping students engaged and on task, minimizing disruptions and maintaining the flow of lessons. This is the purpose of effective classroom management. Many techniques can be employed. Here are a few of the most useful:

1. **Use physical cues and prompts.** Research tells us that teachers usually interrupt their own lessons more than students do. It is the teacher's reaction to student misbehavior that creates this effect. To avoid the problem, use physical cues, usually hand motions, to signal children that they should sit down, avoid interruptions, lower their voices, or be quiet. With young children who are frequently out of their seats, physically redirect them without interrupting your lesson. Similarly, use prompts to redirect them to their work.

2. **Move around the classroom.** Misbehavior quickly escalates in a classroom when the teacher stands in one spot or sits down, particularly if the teacher sits in an out-of-the-way location. To keep students on task, move constantly around the room. Do not stay too long with any one student. Your presence throughout the classroom will prevent the majority of disruptive behaviors.

3. **Genuinely reinforce positive behavior.** It is always worth recognizing desirable behavior. However, students are insightful and they know the difference between sincere praise and insincere manipulation.

Hence, compliment students on answers that are genuinely worthy of praise, the ones that show insight. Thank them for supporting a lesson by being nondisruptive. Take note when the students start to work immediately or cooperate at a higher than usual level. Young children enjoy being praised in front of everybody. They would appreciate it if you would do handstands and cartwheels while calling their name. Older students would die of embarrassment if they were given the same treatment. As students get older, praise them in a quieter, more subtle, and more personal manner.

4. **Get the students' attention before giving directions.** This strategy is one of the most obvious, and most frequently forgotten, strategies. When you want to speak to a group of students, insist that they stop talking and listen. Not only is it more effective, but it is also reinforces the need for courtesy. Also, ensure that your students listen quietly when another student is speaking, especially during presentations.

5. **Modulate your voice.** To keep students interested and attentive, be sure to modulate your voice. The brain learns to block out sounds that are at the same pitch for lengthy periods of time. Sound enthusiastic about the lesson material. Let your personal interest "infect" the students. Once in a while, suddenly raise your voice and be emphatic. When students are becoming noisy, lower your voice. They will be forced to lower theirs in order to hear the lesson and any directions you are giving.

6. **Challenge students to beat the clock.** When you are at home and you have the job of cleaning the house, it can take all day—unless you get a phone call and find out company is arriving in thirty minutes. It is amazing how much work you can get down in a short period of time if you have a deadline to meet. Students are no different. They will put a real burst of energy into their work when there is a challenge such as beating the clock. You could also break the class into teams and have them race each other.

7. **Keep lessons well paced.** It's the information age. In all forms of media, information is being provided in a condensed format that can be absorbed quickly and easily. This has influenced advertising,

television programming, magazines, and newspapers. Teachers cannot be expected to present information in the same way as Bill Nye the Science Guy. Nonetheless, it is essential for lessons to be well paced in order to keep students engaged and attentive. Vary your presentation style, questioning formats, and activities. Insert short quizzes and special challenges.

8. **Keep groups "on a string."** When you are working with a group of students at a table, you would like to be able to give them your undivided attention. At the same time, however, you cannot afford to ignore disruptions elsewhere in the classroom. Here is a great way to do both. Move about the classroom and redirect students to task nonverbally. At the same time, continue to interact verbally with your group of students. As you move around, do so as if you are holding a string that connects you to the center of the group. This forces you to constantly face the group even as you move around the room. By utilizing this technique, you leave the group with the impression that you worked directly with them all the time.

9. **Arrange desks to maximize learning.** Do not put the students' desks into groups at the beginning of the school year. This seating arrangement stimulates a very high level of off-task behavior, particularly conversation. Working effectively in a group is very difficult, even for adults. For this reason, workstations, designed to seat three or four adults, are built with visual dividers. Otherwise, the users would have a very difficult time concentrating. Students have difficulty with these arrangements as well. It takes a great deal of practice and a high level of self-control to be able to work in a group, unless it is for short periods of time. Groupings are fine if they are reserved for specific activities. Start with the desks in rows until students are capable of handling clustered seating arrangements. If the availability of space makes rows impossible, try putting desks together in pairs with both students facing forward. If they are facing each other, they will be talking to each other. There are also many students who find it almost impossible to work in a group, so always have some separate desks as well for those who cannot concentrate in a group environment.

10.   **Provide "sponge" activities.** Develop a wide range of "sponge" activities (so called because they soak up any undirected time) that students may do when they have completed their assigned work. Such activities could include puzzles, high interest reading, mazes, word searches, and so on. Students with idle hands quickly begin to engage in disruptive behaviors. Educational research has consistently confirmed what common sense has already told us. When students have a high rate of on-task behavior, they have a low rate of off-task misbehavior.

11.   **Use "delayed discussion."** Resist the temptation to lecture a student in front of his or her peers. Everyone loses in these situations. Students usually feel embarrassed and may try to save face. Likewise, teachers often feel that their authority is being undermined and respond with threats or punishment. Avoid these situations by making a statement such as, "That is unacceptable. We will talk about it later." Then get on with your lesson. Always make a note to yourself as a reminder to meet with the student. If you forget, then your words become meaningless. Have the meeting in private.

12.   **Remove objects that tend to distract.** Students are often tempted to play with toys and other objects that should be kept out of the way in their desks or backpacks. Many teachers give several warnings before curtailing this disruptive activity. Resist the temptation to deal with this behavior verbally since this only serves to further disrupt the lesson. Instead, remove the object and place it in an appropriate location. Make it clear that the object is being set aside, not confiscated, avoiding unnecessary confrontation and possible infringement of property rights.

13.   **Have students repeat directions.** Do you remember what it was like to sit through a lecture at your university? At any one moment, how many students were listening to the professor? If the professor gave directions for an assignment, how many missed the instructions and had to ask the person sitting next to them? Exactly. When you give directions to your class, assume that some of the students did not get them and do not know what to do. It is not misbehavior on their part—just human nature. Hence, have a couple of students repeat the directions back to you. This is especially important for

ADD students who may not have processed the information even though they heard every word you said.

14. **Use humor.** Humor can defuse the tension of a potentially difficult situation. It stops the escalation of win/lose confrontations without forcing participants to back down. Using humor in the classroom shows students how to relieve the stress involved in everyday life. However, be very careful when using any form of sarcasm. It is easily interpreted as a put-down. Insert humor into lessons to keep pupils aware, involved, and attentive. Use cartoons and occasional nonsense choices on tests to ease the tension. Create a bulletin board display of cartoons and funny photographs. Provide opportunities for students to write captions. Remember to teach students that jokes should be humorous to all concerned. Jokes based on the sensitivities of others cause emotional distress and arouse resentment.

# Building
# Effective
# Discipline

CHAPTER TEN

# Decide in Advance
# How Your Students Will Behave

# Decide in Advance How Your Students Will Behave

*Education is proactive.*
*Teachers make their decisions about curriculum before school starts.*
*They know what their students will be learning*
*long before they even meet the students.*

The same is true for discipline. Teachers who are effective disciplinarians know exactly how their students will behave long before they meet the students. They have a clear picture of how their students will enter the classroom, move to their desks, and get to work. They can visualize assignments being turned in, students working in groups, and so on.

It is important to understand that these teachers visualize positive behavior. They do not waste their time thinking about incidents that might occur and worrying about their ability to respond. They understand that discipline is primarily about how children will behave well, not about how one should react when they do not.

So, decide now. How will your students speak to you and to other students? What tone of voice will they use? What courtesy words will you hear? Unless you can answer these questions, you will not be consistent with your expectations. Neither will you be able to correct errors when they occur.

Let's take a moment and relate this to something totally different. This may seem like an odd comparison, but it is actually quite appropriate. You enter the family room of your house shortly after the last of eight guests has departed. The room is a mess, and it is your job to clean it. What you may not realize is that, as you undertake this job, you actually do a very interesting first step, a step that you are not even aware of. You compare the present state of the room against a vivid picture you hold in your brain of what the room looks like when it is clean. Every difference between the two pictures is a job that needs to be done. You label the jobs (garbage, liquid to be mopped up, etc.) and then start doing them. If it were not for the vivid picture of what the room looks like clean, you would never be able to do the job properly.

Great teachers apply this same principle to their students. They have a vivid, highly detailed picture in their brains of exactly how their students will behave. When the students arrive, every difference between what they see in front of them and what they see in their brain is a job that needs to be done.

If you have children of your own, here is a little insight. When you tell your children to clean a room, they do not have your picture in their brains. Hence, it is impossible for them to do the job exactly the way you wanted it done. They also do not have the same labels. To you, an empty cola can is "garbage"; to your children it is "decoration." If you really need to get the job done properly, help clean the room once and then take a photograph of the room. When it is time to clean it again, just say, "Make it look like this." And one more tidbit—husbands do not have the same picture either.

Here are some questions to help you clarify your picture of how your students will behave. This list of questions is meant to only guide your thinking. It is not intended to be an exhaustive list. Undoubtedly, hundreds of questions could be asked.

### Courtesy
- How will your students speak to you? What tone of voice will they use?
- When you greet them, will they respond in kind?
- How will they speak to other students and to other teachers?
- Will they hold doors open for others?
- How will they treat visitors?
- Do you expect to hear "please" and "thank you" from them?

- Will they be welcoming to new students?
- How will they behave when another student is making a presentation to the class?
- Will they listen when you are speaking?
- Will they wait patiently when you are speaking to others?

## Treatment of Others

- How will your students behave for substitute teachers?
- How will they treat students who are new to the school?
- How will they treat visitors?
- How will they respond to students who need assistance?

## Response to Frustration

- What will they do when they are upset?
- How will they disagree with you or others?
- How will they handle a failing grade?
- How will they deal with losing?

## Response to Authority

- How will your students respond when you correct them?
- Will they comply when you tell them what to do?
- How will they respond to directions from a teacher who is not "one of theirs"?

## Situations

- How will they behave when you step out of the room, have your back turned, or are busy helping an individual or working with a group?
- How will they conduct themselves during assemblies?

## Work Habits

- Will your students complete their assignments?
- Will they work up to their potential?
- Will they willingly improve their work if it is deemed sub-standard?
- How will they deal with mundane tasks?

## Cooperative Play

- Will your students accept others into their games?
- Will they *invite* others into their games?
- How will they handle "getting out" in a game?
- Will they share items with other students?

# CHAPTER ELEVEN

# Design the Supporting Structure

# Design the Supporting Structure

Now that you have a clear picture of how your students will behave, you need to support your efforts by developing a structure of rules, limits, and procedures. As with the questions that you answered in the last chapter, these lists are not exhaustive. They represent a starting point only, and you should be prepared to add to the list. Also, all rules and procedures must be adapted for different grade levels.

**Procedures**

Decide on your procedures for the following:
- Entering and exiting
- Arriving late
- Going to learning centers and work stations
- Handing in work and exchanging work
- Moving from one classroom to another
- Asking and answering questions
- Requesting assistance
- Working with peers
- Sharpening pencils
- Borrowing materials from peers
- Going to the restroom
- Handing out playground materials
- Doing activities prior to morning announcements or opening exercises
- Finding assignments missed due to absence
- Finishing work early
- Responding appropriately if the teacher has not arrived

**Classroom Rules**

- Come to class prepared to work
- Arrive on time
- Complete your work
- Allow others to get their work done

**Limits and Restrictions**

No violence is allowed, including the following:
- Physical hitting
- Bullying
- Threatening and intimidating
- Sexual assault
- Insults and taunting

No weapons

No academic dishonesty (cheating, submitting papers purchased through the Internet, copying work from a textbook, etc.)

Do not play a game with students by allowing them to make up classroom rules. Students are supposed to learn about school rules, not determine them. Teach them why we have rules, explain the role of authority, and discuss decisions that are made by people in positions of authority. You could have them create a theoretical set of rules and then compare their rules to the real ones. You can take their opinions into account in the creation of rules and even in the design of the code of conduct. Just do not pretend that their rules are the ones that count. After all, when students are old enough to drive, they will not be allowed to make up their own rules of the road.

CHAPTER TWELVE

# Establish a Clear Threshold

# Establish a Clear Threshold

To ensure effective discipline in school, you must not allow students to bring negative home and community behaviors and attitudes into the learning environment. You must create a clear separation, a dividing line, between school and the outside world to communicate to students, "You're now at school. Remember how you behave when you're here."

The management approach does not create this separation. With management, you work with whatever behaviors and attitudes the students bring with them. After observing the nature of your students, you encourage their appropriate behaviors and discourage the inappropriate ones. With discipline, on the other hand, you create a set of school behaviors that is activated when students enter the environment and deactivated when they leave. For individual classroom teachers who are establishing quality discipline on their own, the most effective threshold is usually the classroom door.

For school discipline, there are two possible thresholds. The first is established at the school doors, and it is the easiest to enforce. The second option has a far greater impact on school culture but is more difficult to enforce. This option involves establishing the school grounds as the threshold.

Here are the key steps involved in creating this effect that is crucial for the development of situational discipline.

**Be Clear About Which Behaviors Will Be Excluded**

You must know in advance which behaviors and attitudes you will disallow and which you will accept. To exclude behaviors from the school as a whole, decisions must be made as a staff and authorized by administration. They must conform with district policies and should be clearly communicated to both parents and staff.

Obviously, you do not want violence, gangs, drugs, and weapons anywhere in the learning environment. Even so, the decision making now becomes more difficult. Are you prepared to exclude the gang clothing and symbols that are a basic element of membership in gangs and cults? Do you intend to scan for weapons and bring in drug-sniffing dogs? How will you deal with cults and other special groups that focus on violence and antisocial behavior? Do you intend to prohibit sexually provocative behavior? What about provocative clothing? Then what will you do about violent images on kids' shirts and on student binders? Will surliness be tolerated (the general "chip-on-the-shoulder" angry attitude that some students bring from home)? There are a lot of decisions to make. Make sure you are willing and able to follow through on them.

**Be There to Make It Happen**

Creating a threshold requires a high level of adult supervision. If you want to block certain behaviors from entering your classroom, you have to be at the classroom door when the students are arriving. For school discipline, teachers must cover the school grounds, particularly first thing in the morning and after lunch. They must also be covering all general entry points. If a student gets his inappropriate behavior past one teacher, every other teacher needs to be ready to stop him. There are no shortcuts in real discipline.

**"Not Here!"**

Next, you must be willing to assertively reject behaviors that are not allowed in the school environment. This is not a comfortable task for many teachers. However, if it is done quietly and confidently, and if students are allowed to maintain their dignity, then confrontations should be rare. Research suggests that it takes approximately three years to change the culture of a school, so be prepared to maintain your efforts. Eventually, most students will stop pushing the limits and realize that certain behaviors are simply not acceptable at school.

## Be Prepared to Follow Through

Once you have assertively stated that a particular behavior will not be tolerated, you must be prepared to follow through. There is no "give" on threshold behaviors. If a student's t-shirt has unacceptable graphics on it, have him go directly to the office to obtain a cover-up shirt. If a student's surly attitude is unacceptable, ensure that there is a supervised location where the student can go until he or she is ready for classroom learning. Having a clear threshold does not mean that you suspend every student who is not ready to enter the school. You do not want the student to go home; you want the student ready to go to class. Ensure that there are school-based solutions to most violations.

You will also find yourself explaining your threshold rules to parents who perceive the "absolute" nature of the rules as unreasonable. You will frequently experience pressure from parents to allow the child's behavior "just this one time." No means no. Many potential problems with parents can be avoided by communicating with them in advance of any problems.

CHAPTER
THIRTEEN

# Run a Two-Week Training Camp

# Run a Two-Week Training Camp

*The investment you make in discipline during
the first two weeks of school determines
how the rest of the school year will unfold.*

Professional sports teams start each season with a training camp. Every day, the coaches make the players practice various skills that will be essential for success during the season. They also run drills that are designed to train players to respond automatically in various situations. In addition, players learn to respond to instructions from coaches without arguing. During the season, if the team goes into a slump, they get back to the "fundamentals" by having a mini-training camp. Through this camp, the coaches re-establish routines that have been lost over time. If training camps are important for highly paid athletes who are at the peak of their professional abilities, then they are certainly important for students.

Good teachers do exactly the same thing. They run training camps in their classrooms for the first two weeks of each school year, and they do so for the same reasons that professional teams do so. It allows them to establish clear limits and expectations, train students to follow routines and comply, and teach students how to behave appropriately.

Unfortunately, many teachers are presently skipping this vital component of discipline, and not just because the concept of training camp is not part of classroom management. It is also because teachers in today's schools are trying to cope with extraordinary curriculum demands. As a result, many of them choose to focus on academics immediately, feeling that there is simply no time to waste. However, if students are to work together and play together successfully, they must first learn to work within the structure of the classroom and school, obey rules, follow procedures, and comply with directions.

If there is a rule that governs priorities, it is *compliance before cooperation*. This rule does not mean that academics are overlooked for the first two weeks. It is simply a matter of priorities. Learning to work efficiently and socialize appropriately are the top priorities for this time period. Academics come second, although they are still important and a great deal of work should still be accomplished. What good teachers have found over the years is that any time spent on discipline during the first two weeks is repaid many times over. You will be able to accomplish curriculum goals better if you establish effective discipline first.

The guidelines below should be followed during the first two weeks of school:

- Establish clear limits and rules. Communicate them to students assertively. Make statements such as, "Be on time" rather than, "If you are late, you will have a detention." Remember that this last sentence communicates a choice, not a rule.

- Be "warm strict." Strict does not mean punitive or unfriendly. It means you have "tight" limits and expectations that you enforce consistently. "Warm" means that you establish a positive rapport with your students.

- Train students to follow classroom procedures.

- Teach transitions so they run efficiently. Classroom transitions such as switching from one subject to another, handing in test papers, or gathering in groups should take an average of sixty to ninety seconds. Entry and exit transitions should take approximately two to three minutes (except when young children have to get into winter clothing). Time the transitions and challenge the students to get the time down to a preset goal.

- Teach students their essential skills, starting with courtesy. Courtesy helps establish cooperative interactions between the students that are important for the smooth functioning of the learning environment.

*Remember to employ a very high level of supervision during the first two weeks of school.*

# CHAPTER FOURTEEN

# Teach Students to Behave Appropriately

# Teach Students to Behave Appropriately

Many of our students arrive at school without the skills necessary for responsible and cooperative behavior. Sometimes, it is because the parents do not have the time, the inclination, or the ability to take on this task. Other parents do not teach their children how to behave correctly because they have bought into behavior management. They think their children will learn correct behavior from personal experience.

The reasons do not matter. Teachers simply have to accept the fact that if they want their students to behave correctly, they will have to teach them to do so. Remember, you do not need to change the timetable and squeeze in some social skills lessons. Almost all skills are best taught in ordinary, everyday interactions between teachers and students, not out of a binder.

There are countless skills for children of all grades to learn. In kindergarten, they must be taught how to sit in a group without annoying those around them. In higher grades, they must be taught conflict resolution and self-discipline. Other skills are listed below:
- Greeting others
- Giving compliments
- Listening quietly when someone is speaking
- Being punctual
- Inviting someone to join in a game
- Sharing

There are hundreds of skills. If you want complete lists, you may wish to consult a social skills program. For the most part, however, it is best to work from your vision of how you want your students to behave.

Below are ten special skills that can make a big difference in your classroom and school. They focus on the development of positive values, cooperative interactions, and self-discipline. Self-discipline is, of course, the major goal.

**Ten Great Skills to Teach Your Students**

### 1. Courtesy

Everyone complains about the lack of courtesy these days, but nobody takes the time to teach it or insist on it. For example, when you hold a door open for a student, do you require the student to say "thank you"? Very few teachers do. Parents also tend to ignore these small transgressions, perhaps expecting courtesy to develop by accident. It will not.

Regardless of the lack of courtesy in the world at large, we should at least insist on it in school. Courtesy is the foundation of cooperative interactions between people. The following are some of the most important skills:
- Greeting others
- Giving and receiving compliments
- Letting someone go ahead of you (whenever appropriate)
- Holding a door open for others
- Saying please and thank you
- Acknowledging a good effort on someone else's part
- Listening when someone is talking
- Offering to help with a job
- Inviting someone to join a game or group

### 2. How to Treat Substitute Teachers

Being a substitute teacher must be one of the most difficult jobs in the world. Far too many students see the presence of a substitute as an opportunity to misbehave. Effective discipline teaches students to show respect to everyone within a classroom or school.

Teach students your expectation that they are to behave just as well for anyone else as they do for you. Then teach them appropriate guest-greeting skills, including how to make someone feel welcome and how to provide assistance as required.

Split your class into groups and train the groups to do various jobs. One group takes on the responsibility for welcoming a substitute, getting any materials required, and showing the substitute where things are located. This group also takes charge of opening exercises. Assign each of the other groups a specific subject or period of the day. Their job is to ensure that everything runs smoothly. Instead of doing the work themselves, they are responsible for taking charge of groups, working with students who need extra help, handing out and collecting materials, explaining directions, and doing peer tutoring.

After the training is completed, arrange a practice session. Trade places with another teacher, one your students rarely deal with, and instruct your students to act as if the teacher is a substitute. If this skill is being taught across an entire school, schedule a time when all the teachers can switch places for half a day or even a full day.

Your substitute teachers will be overjoyed at receiving such a high level of support. The number of incidents will plummet, and your students will have learned a host of great leadership skills along the way. *Then, why not change the word "subs" to "guest teachers"?*

## 3. Conflict Prevention

Behavior management is reactive. As a result, there are hundreds of books and programs on the market focusing on conflict resolution—what to do after a conflict has developed. Try to find even one book on conflict prevention—how to ensure that a conflict does not develop in the first place.

Help your students recognize the events that lead up to various incidents and to problem solve alternative ways of avoiding the situations. Have them devise methods for ensuring positive outcomes.

Teach your students to identify the following:
  • Good playmates

- Peers they work well with
- Games they can play without incident
- People and situations they should avoid

Teach them how to do the following:
- Respond to teasing with humor or reciprocation
- Ignore irritants (actually a difficult response to learn)
- "Walk off" their anger, or utilize some other appropriate means of relieving frustration
- Know the difference between reciprocation and escalation so they can avoid making tense situations any worse
- Involve a teacher or peer mediator before a problem occurs so it does not occur

## 4. Self-Discipline

When children are very young, adults are required to exert a great deal of control over them in order to ensure correct behavior. The long-term goal, of course, is to have children learn the skill of self-discipline. We want them to be able to control themselves and behave appropriately without constant adult supervision. This skill does not develop by itself. It must be taught and modeled.

With young children, start by teaching them that self-discipline is the ability to make the same decisions when they are unsupervised as they would have made if an adult were standing next to them. If an incident occurs, do not ask why they misbehaved; ask whether they would have acted the same way if you had been there. Almost invariably, the answer will be "no." Your next question is, "Why do you need me standing next to you for you to make a good choice?"

This line of reasoning can be instilled ahead of time as well. When children want to go somewhere on their own, ask them how they would behave if you went with them. Then ask if they are capable of behaving the same without you.

With older students, focus on issues of self-control and self-restraint. These are the ability to say "no" to oneself in various situations where there is temptation to do something wrong.

Additional skills include controlling one's anger and handling minor frustrations without "blowing up."

## 5. Concentration

Remember when students were expected to work quietly? Noise was discouraged because it interfered with student concentration. No longer! Now, students are active and involved. They often work cooperatively, which requires constant discussion. At the same time, other students may be doing activities at various centers around the room, acting as peer tutors to their classmates, or preparing for a special event. This kind of environment can present serious problems for students who are easily distracted.

Concentration can be improved significantly through practice. Make a game out of it by deliberately trying to distract students while they are working on a task. Challenge them to keep their eyes on their work at all times. Use a timer to track their progress. Once they are able to handle this situation, increase the challenge by enlisting the help of several other students who will also attempt to distract their peers. They may call the names of students, bump their elbows, and anything else that normally occurs in a classroom setting. Hitting and name-calling are not permitted.

You will be amazed at how skillful the students will become at ignoring distractions. Of course, once they learn to do so in the game situation, the next challenge is to generalize the behavior across the rest of the school day.

## 6. Be Part of the Solution, Not Part of the Problem

As a teacher, you have undoubtedly been in a situation in which you were required to break up a fight on school grounds. The fight itself is clearly unacceptable. But what about the behavior of students who are standing around watching the fight? Often, their conduct is nothing short of atrocious. They encourage the fighters to continue and even make suggestions for further violence.

It does not always happen this way. There are schools where the students actively attempt to break up the combatants. They usually do so with words by making statements such as, "Hey Joey, Mike. Come on, guys. Break it up. Let's go do something else." Since peer pressure is so powerful, peers can often stop fights more quickly than teachers can. The school and its personnel determine whether students aggravate an already difficult situation or attempt to stop the conflict. It is part of school culture and schoolwide expectations, instilled from the first time students set foot on the school grounds. If you want your students to practice peer intervention, teach them how to do it. Then back it up with your expectations. The next time there is an incident on the grounds, deal seriously with the actions of the surrounding group. Either congratulate them for doing a great job or find out why they did not. Ask them why, when you needed their help with this situation, they did not lend a hand.

There are many other ways children can be part of the solution as well. In classrooms, students can assist other students with their learning, loan items required for the completion of an assignment, or stop hurtful gossip and notes. They can keep the school looking great by taking care of litter. They can make suggestions for beautifying the hallways, cafeteria, and grounds. They can help organize special events.

There are literally hundreds of possibilities. Teachers should not be the only ones finding solutions to problems. In a learning community, everyone is supposed to do his or her part, including the students.

### 7. Think About Others
Children have a very natural tendency to focus on themselves. This tendency is exacerbated when children are constantly offered rewards even for doing simple tasks. For example, look at how common it is for parents to pay allowance in exchange for the completion of chores. In the past, parents required children to do chores as a means of teaching them to be contributors within the family environment. Now, this sense of contribution is often missing.

Children have to be taught to consider others. Help students recognize opportunities to help others. At the end of each day, ask a couple of students to identify who they helped that day and what they contributed to the class or school. Use shared rewards. Students can earn a reward for a group or for the entire class.

Provide a student with two or three rewards and require him to give the extra ones to other students. This type of strategy avoids the selfishness that often accompanies individual rewards.

When a student is having difficulty staying on task or having a good recess, enlist the assistance of the other students. We teach them to help each other with math and reading, so why not with behavior? Establish a peer tutors program and teach participants how to tutor other students, either at the same grade level or in lower grades. Have older students teach playground games to younger students, supervise the games, and arrange competitions. A reading buddies program is easy to design and valuable for all. The social connections are as important as the academic growth. Most of all, focus on the small daily opportunities to include someone in a game, welcome a newcomer, help someone do a job, let someone go first, offer sympathy to someone who is sad, or compliment someone who has done a good job. Programs are great, but it is the small stuff that dramatically changes the culture of a school.

## 8. Perseverance

In today's world, children are surrounded by activities, both at home and at school. If they get bored with one activity, they quickly switch to another. Switching from one activity to another may keep them busy, but it certainly does not teach perseverance, which is the ability to stick with a task even when the novelty has worn off, an important skill in the higher school grades and in the world of work.

Starting in early childhood programs, children should be required to complete some teacher-assigned tasks every day. They must not be allowed to quit or change tasks merely due to a lack of interest. It is often worthwhile to identify tasks that are likely to be mundane and review the need for perseverance before students begin their work.

You may even wish to teach this skill by creating a game. Have students help you design "the world's most boring tasks." Then, challenge them to accomplish the tasks, forcing them to practice their perseverance skills. When students come to you and complain that their assignment is boring, respond by telling them to apply their skills for doing boring work.

### 9. Be a Good Role Model

Children learn many of their behaviors by watching the actions of others, including older siblings, friends, parents, and teachers. Then they imitate whatever they observed. Therefore, it is very important for older children to understand the impact they have on anyone younger than they are. You will often hear parents scolding a child for doing something inappropriate while a younger sibling is watching.

In the school environment, we tend to overlook the importance of this type of interaction, mostly because students are clustered into similar age groupings. If every class had cross-age groupings, teachers would immediately reinstate the expectation that students should adjust their behavior in the presence of younger children. Nonetheless, this concept can still be applied to common areas and is particularly important in elementary school settings.

Teach students to consider their choice of words, jokes, body language, and conversation topics when they are in the presence of younger children. Since this skill is mostly required for hallways and playgrounds, remember to supervise the students during these times and direct their behaviors.

Students should also model compliance with school routines and procedures such as forming lines. For example, even if older students have been granted the privilege of entering a different door where they do not have to line up, they should recognize the importance of doing so whenever the situation changes and younger students are forming their lines in the same area.

### 10. Ambassadors

Your students are your ambassadors. How they present themselves in public reflects on every aspect of your school, including the academic program. When your students behave well and dress appropriately, people in the community quickly conclude that the students must be from a great school with great teachers and great programs. People in the community draw this conclusion even if they have never visited the school. Such is the power of creating an impression.

Unfortunately, children tend to be so self-centered that they rarely consider the impression their behavior leaves on others—unless you teach them the concept. There are some real benefits to teaching this concept because it also gives you a way of demanding high-quality behavior without appearing arbitrary and unreasonable. After all, it is not for you, it is to make the school look good. Make sure that you also apply these expectations for student behavior around school visitors.

### Running a Social Skills Group?

When a few students are selected for inclusion in a social skills group, everybody knows why, including the students themselves. To protect their dignity and improve the effectiveness of their learning, try employing a "train the trainers" model. Teach the small group of students how to teach the social skills to an entire class of younger students. Doing so will consolidate their own skills, raise their self-esteem, and of course, benefit the younger students as well. Everyone wins.

# Making
# It
# Work

# CHAPTER FIFTEEN

# Set the Stage

# Set the Stage

*Discipline works best when it is done in conjunction
with other elements of quality education.
Think of discipline as having "partners."*

## A Challenging, Engaging Program

The first "partner" is the provision of a meaningful, challenging, and engaging program. Discipline cannot succeed in an environment where students are faced with boring, tedious lessons and activities. In the past, such lessons were not unusual in schools. Teachers could get away with it back then because the discipline techniques of the day were designed to keep students passive. In addition, school was the most exciting thing in the lives of many children, despite tedious lessons. Teachers only had to compete with the desire of students to play and daydream.

*The world has changed.* For better or worse, the world is now information-rich and highly stimulating. Television programs are fast-paced and graphically intense. Video games are complex and engaging. Even the producers of advertisements have changed the content dramatically in an effort to attract attention. In this kind of world, a day full of tedious lessons is like a daylong root canal. There is no way anyone would sit still for it. Here are some guidelines for developing a challenging, engaging program:

- Design your lessons to be interesting and challenging.

- Ask questions that force students to expand their thinking into unusual areas.

- Develop hands-on activities.

- Design assignments to be just a little more difficult than students think they can accomplish.

- Apply concepts to everyday experiences. For instance, teach the students about money by having them purchase materials from a catalog in anticipation of a theoretical camping trip.

- Integrate various subject areas together.

- Design group-learning activities that require students to develop a wide variety of skills including interviewing, research, and analysis.

- In addition to having students present research projects to their own classmates, have them do presentations for students in lower grades.

- Arrange out-of-school trips to extend the curriculum and provide opportunities for the development of independence.

- Integrate technology into the curriculum. Include audio and visual technologies in addition to the use of computers. Be creative. For instance, students are now able to compose music by combining computers and keyboards. There is literally no end to the possibilities in this field.

- Develop cross-graded activities. All students benefit by working with other students of different ages.

- Develop work-experience opportunities. Local businesses may be very willing to support efforts in this regard.

### Invitational Environment

The world is a colorful, exciting place full of unique people and places. There is always something new and interesting to investigate. Walking into a dingy school and spending your day in a barren classroom is, at best, discouraging.

- Put student art into proper frames and hang the artwork in the hallways.

- Schedule special days that allow students to show their creativity.

- Decorate the classroom with fascinating items, puzzles, and brainteasers, in addition to student work and projects. Do not pay attention to the old maxim that a boring room is less distracting. Tedious environments simply encourage children to create their own visual landscapes in their imaginations, and thus they will be daydreaming instead of working. It is better for them to be looking at meaningful material.

- Have the school crest and mascot painted on walls both inside and outside the school.

- Announce school events and special news on lighted signboards outside the school.

- Survey parents to find out which ones have special abilities. Involve them in special projects such as painting undersea scenes on the library walls. Older students may wish to paint murals on the walls of the cafeteria (subject to authorization).

- Put groups of students in charge of designing bulletin board displays. They do a fabulous job, especially if you provide them with a couple of resource books that show ideas for decorating the boards.

**Extracurricular Activities**

Schools are intended to do more than simply develop children's academic abilities. Extracurricular activities provide opportunities for social growth and the development of a wide range of life skills. Design a wide variety of activities to ensure that every student has the opportunity to be involved in at least one area of personal interest. Here are some examples:

- Include activities based on sports, music, intellectual challenges, drama, crafts, and games.

- Enlist community volunteers to run groups, especially for crafts, and games such as chess.

- Design activities to run for a relatively short period of time (3–6 sessions). These include specific crafts, cooking (make your own pizza), or a challenge contest in a game such as Trivial Pursuit.

**Classroom "Engineering"**

Many discipline problems can be avoided by carefully considering the design of your classroom in regard to desks, working areas, and learning centers.

- Start the year by placing desks in rows or pairs rather than groups. Students should all be facing you initially, limiting conversation that naturally results from clustered seating arrangements.

- Allow easy access to areas where assignments are picked up and submitted, "sponge" activities are stored, and personal materials (jackets, lunches, backpacks) are stored. Also, provide direct access to the pencil sharpener.

- Position your desk so that you are able to maintain eye contact with the students if you choose to sit at the desk for a few minutes during class time.

- Position learning and work centers so they do not interfere with the free movement of students around the classroom. Ensure that some of the work centers are located in quiet areas so they may be used by students who have difficulty concentrating.

CHAPTER SIXTEEN

# Provide Active, Assertive Supervision

# Provide Active, Assertive Supervision

Management strategies focus on how teachers should respond to incidents. Notice it says, "respond," not "prevent." The prevention of incidents would require a significant level of adult control, and it would go against the management philosophy. Unfortunately, the desire to prevent incidents has led to a situation in which many teachers now supervise playgrounds by standing in one spot, watching students misbehave, and then doing something in response. In fact, this is not supervision at all. Standing in one spot and watching how students conduct themselves is called "monitoring." Discipline requires *supervision,* which is a proactive process used to ensure that students *do not* misbehave. Teachers are there to prevent problems. To monitor effectively, it is necessary to move around the area, establish a presence, and direct students in an assertive, non-confrontational manner. Make sure you attend to all students, not just the ones in your class or grade.

It is often necessary to go "above and beyond" the basic supervision schedule. There are great, long-lasting benefits to providing extra supervision during the first two weeks of school. Also, ensure that there is coverage at the beginning of the school day, even if it is not required by your teaching contract. This supervision is essential if you are going to establish a threshold and have students switch over to their school behaviors. Administrators must also provide a visible supervisory presence on the grounds and in the hallways of a school. Leadership is important.

**They Are** *Never* **Too Old**

One of the most serious deficiencies in today's discipline is the tendency for teachers to believe that older students need very little supervision. Supervision has nothing to do with age; it has to do with what you are trying to accomplish. If you were fifty years old, didn't know how to drive, and went for driver training, the instructor would still sit right next to you in the car, the same way it would be done for a sixteen-year-old.

The issue of supervision for adolescents is that it should be *nonintrusive, not nonexistent.* You should give them some room to spread their wings, but you still have to be there to get the job done.

Below are some key strategies for effective supervision.

**Proximity**

- Move briskly around the entire supervision area. Talk briefly to students but avoid staying in one area and talking to a single group.

- Assess the area and know where the trouble spots are. Move quickly toward groups of students who are loud, boisterous, or beginning to engage in rough play. Also, watch for students congregating in secluded areas. Provide extra coverage to these areas.

- To supervise the school grounds, consider using devices that extend the range of your influence. Whistles get attention far more effectively than yelling. Vests make you more visible, although they also allow students to easily know when you are not in the vicinity.

- Be outside promptly. Many incidents occur as students are heading out the doors. Avoid going to the staff room prior to heading outside. If you wish to have a drink outside with you, arrange for another teacher to bring it to you. Ensure that the cup has a lid so you can move around the grounds without worrying about spilling your drink.

- Similarly, when students are in the hallways, ensure that you are out there with them. Whenever possible, escort them between classrooms.

## Assertive Presence

- Move with a sense of purpose. For outside areas, use a brisk, steady stride that conveys a "no-nonsense" approach and indicates that you are in charge. Stand up straight, keep your head up, and make eye contact with students. Calm, controlled movements convey authority.

- Use an assertive tone of voice. (If you do not have one, work on it.) Be firm and authoritative. Tone, cadence, and volume can communicate more than the actual words that are spoken. Remember that calmness is contagious.

- Always attempt to deal with the problem personally. Students need to learn to behave for the teachers, not for the principal. Many management strategies rely on power, most of which is maintained by administration. Discipline relies on authority, which is vested in every teacher in a school (plus the secretary, custodial staff, etc.).

## Assertive Communication and Direction

- Remind students of rules and expectations before there are problems so there will not be any problems. If necessary, ask them to repeat the rules to you.

- Communicate limits by using statements such as, "No hitting." Remember that saying, "If you hit, you will go to the principal's office" actually provides students with a choice.

- Redirect students when they are beginning to engage in activities that you know may lead to problems.

- Be specific and statement-oriented. Avoid over-verbalizing.

- Don't let students "wind your crank." Use the "broken record technique," restating your expectations and directions.

- Govern and correct small misbehaviors before they become big ones. Remember, behavior you ignore is behavior you permit.

- Reinforce positive social skills when you see them being used. Also, reinforce respect for authority and rules.

- When students are just beginning to "lose it," have them walk with you rather than sending them to stand against the wall or fence. Remember that the issue is how children will behave appropriately. If they are having trouble doing so on their own, then they can do it within your supervisory radius.

# CHAPTER SEVENTEEN

# Enforce Rules and Expectations

# Enforce Rules and Expectations

So great is our reliance on consequences that most teachers now believe consequences are the basis for enforcement. When they are dealing with students, they issue constant warnings about the consequences that will result from certain actions. Many schools go to great lengths to write codes of conduct that list specific consequences for specific actions. Although consequences are important, they are not the centerpiece of discipline. While behavior management relies on consequences, discipline relies on authority.

**Insistence Pays Off**

With authority, you enforce your rules and directions by assertively following through and insisting that your students do what you tell them to do. For instance, if you tell a student to sit quietly for ten minutes while you read a story to the class, then sooner or later, the student must do precisely that. If you direct a student to finish an assignment, you must be willing to invest the time and effort necessary to insist that the job be completed. Failure to do so undermines your authority. *It is your ability to require good behavior that will determine your eventual success.*

This concept may sound simple, but it is not. It requires a significant shift on the part of many teachers. First, you must be willing to take charge of students and establish the authority that is a natural function of the teaching role. This authority has decreased steadily over the years, and not just because of changes in society. Understand the impact of using, for twenty years, a system of discipline that employs negotiation and bargaining techniques. There is no authority in this system. *With behavior management, teachers* encourage *students to behave appropriately. With discipline, teachers* require *students to behave appropriately.*

With discipline, you do not play games with students, pretending they are allowed to make up the classroom rules. You do not let them call you by your first name, pretending you are a friend of theirs. And you certainly do not allow them to misbehave in the classroom, talking back to you, running around, or throwing things at other students. You must take charge of the classroom.

## Establish Authority Right from the Start

Establish authority from the very first moment your students arrive at the classroom door. When you greet them, make certain that they return your greeting. Under no circumstances should you let a student walk past and ignore you. The simple act of stopping students and insisting they reciprocate sends a clear message that they are entering a classroom where courtesy and respect will be required, not just appreciated. Think about it. It is the first day of school, they still have their jackets and backpacks on, and they already know who is in charge and what will be expected of them.

## The Role of the Principal

To establish authority and enforce your rules, you must change your perception of the role of the principal. With management techniques, the principal is the big threat because administrators are able to use the biggest consequences. This method results in a multitude of students being sent to the principal's office for "discipline."

Real discipline, on the other hand, builds authority, and this authority is vested in every staff member (including teaching assistants, secretaries, caretakers, bus drivers, etc.), not just with administrators. Students must learn to do what any staff member tells them to do, not just what the principal tells them to do. In fact, transferring the problem to the principal often undermines authority instead of building it. *The role of the principal is to support teacher authority, not to replace it.*

Implementing real discipline does not mean that you never send a student to the office. It simply means that you do not transfer the problem to someone else. For instance, suppose a student constantly interrupts your lesson. You do everything possible to settle him, including using proximity, nonverbal cues, and assertive communication about desired behavior. But nothing works. At this point, your concern is for the rights and needs of the other students who are sitting there ready to learn. Hence, you instruct the disruptive student to proceed to the office. This action is absolutely appropriate. All the studies of effective schools indicate that teachers must protect the integrity of their lessons.

However, do not have the principal deal with the student. Instead, arrange for the principal to support your efforts by supervising the student until you have time to retrieve him. Then, take the time to insist that the student do exactly what you told him to do—sit quietly and listen to a lesson. Doing so builds your authority and enforces your directions. If the student is rude or defiant, you may need to add in a consequence that will give the student the message that "no means no." However, do not forget—when the consequence is over, he must still proceed to do what he was told to do. It is your tenacious persistence, the essence of being strict, that will eventually make a difference. Strict does not mean punitive; it means consistently firm. Remember to lower your voice and enunciate your words whenever you need to be assertive. Yelling denotes a loss of control.

### Worried About Confrontations?

Many teachers worry about having confrontations with students when they enforce rules and expectations. To avoid experiencing major problems with confrontations, make sure you enforce your directions on very small behaviors first, including ensuring that students hang up their jackets correctly, speak courteously, and clean up items around their desks. Ensuring that students follow your directions is not about being "picky." It is about teaching students that you mean what you say. If you teach this lesson on small behaviors, you will not have to teach it on the big behaviors, at least not very often.

Let's relate this idea to parenting for a moment. Ineffective parents often worry about whether their children will be home by a specified time. They wonder how they should respond if curfew is violated. Effective parents do not worry. They know their children will obey the rules. What makes the difference? Effective parents teach their children to obey parental rules and directions by following through on small behaviors like picking up toys, making beds, doing chores, and going to bed on time. The children learn that their parents mean what they say on small issues and apply it to big issues. As a result, lessons do not have to be taught on big behaviors such as curfew. Follow this principle in your classroom. If you govern the small behaviors, most of the big behaviors will fall into place.

### And If They Do Not?

When big behaviors do occur, it is still important to follow through. If you told a student to go to the office and he needs assistance in getting there, then be prepared to physically intervene. Request assistance if necessary. If you are concerned about the ramifications of touching a student, read the box at the end of this chapter and see the follow-up material in the appendix.

Keep in mind that you need to follow through, but you do not always have to follow through immediately. You can often delay your intervention to a time that is more convenient to you, just as long as there are not any safety issues involved in the situation. If you intend to delay intervention, make sure you inform the offending student that his behavior is unacceptable and that you will deal with him later. Otherwise, you would appear to be permitting his behavior.

### Make a Positive Connection

Earlier in this chapter, you were warned about the danger of trying to elicit appropriate student behavior by being friends with students. You should, however, establish rapport. The difference is that rapport means being friendly, not friends. It is a big difference.

Developing rapport is about connecting with students in a positive way, which allows students to interpret the intent of your actions. Hence, they interpret your enforcement as an attempt to help them, not to control them. When students believe you are trying to influence them for positive reasons, they will generally avoid confronting you in response to your rules and directions.

- Listen to your students and take their concerns into account.

- Integrate your students' interests into the program.

- Use humor. It is a great relationship builder.

- Wipe the slate clean after incidents. Constantly reminding students about past problems is a sure way of destroying rapport.

- Keep incidents in perspective. Students will make mistakes, so do not act as if it is the end of the civilized world. Remember that teaching goes on forever.

- When a student is going through a difficult time outside of school, be understanding and supportive. There is a time for indicating that an assignment need not be completed. Even better, perhaps you could complete it yourself, mark it "Excellent" (what else?), and return it to the student—a true gift from the heart!

Combining insistence with rapport gives you what you really want—"warm strict"—all the benefits of being strict combined with all the benefits of establishing a positive relationship with students.

### Not Allowed to Touch Students?

One of the more disturbing trends in education has been the undermining of teacher authority by those who seek to avoid conflict at any cost. In particular, teachers in many jurisdictions have been advised not to touch students because this action could prompt a lawsuit.

Let's establish, once and for all, that physical contact with students is an inherent part of an educator's job. The issue is not whether it will occur, but whether it will be professional and appropriate. Included in the appendices of this book is a copy of the Lincoln County Board of Education's physical intervention procedures and guidelines. The board recognizes that "contact is considered appropriate provided that it reflects the constructive nature of effective teaching and discipline techniques." Additional techniques are authorized for safety purposes. Physical intervention for punitive purposes is forbidden. After reviewing the guidelines, Family and Children's Services (which deals with child protection) advised the board that it supported the policy. Further, it would consider a teacher's refusal to implement these

procedures to be a violation of the Child Welfare Act.
As professionals, we are not allowed to decline to do our jobs.

For someone to suggest that teachers should not touch kids is like the firefighters' union advising their members not to go near burning buildings or the police officers' union advising officers not to arrest suspects because they could get sued. Teachers need clear and unequivocal support from administration. It is a difficult job at the best of times. When enforcement and control procedures are required, teachers need to know how to respond in a professional manner and should receive administrative support for doing so.

# CHAPTER EIGHTEEN

# Focus on Prevention

# Focus on Prevention

Remember the difference in beliefs between management and discipline. Management is based on the premise that children should be allowed to make their own choices. Adults are expected to develop effective responses to whatever behaviors children may choose. Management is inherently reactive. Discipline is proactive. Until children are ready to make choices responsibly, adults take charge and make the choices for them, preventing many of the incidents that are commonly associated with the management approach.

Hence, discipline is not what you do when children misbehave. It is what you do so they will not misbehave. This concept applies to all strategies. Supervision is used to prevent problems, not simply to deal with them after they have already occurred. Rules and limits are established so children will understand that some behaviors are strictly out-of-bounds.

Here are some ideas to help you prevent incidents:

- When your insight into your students tells you that a particular student cannot behave appropriately for substitute teachers, do not wait for the situation to break down. Move the student to another teacher's class before the substitute arrives. Remember, discipline is mostly based on insights, not incidents.

- Since one physical education teacher cannot supervise two change rooms, one for boys and one for girls, arrange for another person, such as a caretaker or a teaching assistant, to provide assistance for this task. This supervision will prevent many problems. Change rooms are often favorite locations for bullying.

- Have impulsive students preplan their recesses. Before they go outside, they should tell you what they are going to do, with whom, where, and who has the equipment. "Joey and I are playing baseball over by the fence, and he has the bat and ball." With a plan in place, the student does not have to interfere with someone else's game in order to get involved.

- Keep students engaged in learning. Every additional minute of on-task behavior is one less minute of off-task behavior, and therefore, one less opportunity for students to misbehave. Remember the saying, "Idle hands are the devil's workshop."

- Provide lots of "sponge" activities to soak up extra time, especially for those students who finish their work early.

- Teach at the correct level of difficulty, not so hard that students cannot accomplish the task but not so easy that they become bored.

- If you are thinking of sending a student to see the principal, try doing it before a problem develops so the principal can make sure it does not. This action supports your efforts. Having the principal intervene after it is too late simply frustrates everyone.

- Stop "put-downs." Verbal hits usually precede physical hits.

- Have your physical education teacher spend some time at the beginning of the school year teaching playground games. In this age of computers and television, it is surprising how many children have no idea how to play the most basic games.

- When you are supervising the school grounds and you see a student just beginning to "lose it," have him walk with you rather than sending him to stand against the wall or fence. Remember, the issue is how children will behave appropriately. If they are having trouble doing so on their own, then they can do it within your supervisory radius.

- Do not let discipline disappear during the lunch hour. Ensure that there is sufficient structure and supervision in place to govern the behavior of students who eat lunch at school. Allowing chaos during lunch sets up the teachers for an exhausting and frustrating afternoon. Supervision is not convenient, but it is necessary.

- For students who cannot concentrate in group situations, provide them with personal work areas before problems develop, not after the problems have already occurred.

- If you have a special area where students hang their coats and one student constantly has problems handling the situation, send him before or after the other students. Do likewise for students who are causing problems on the way home from school. Delay their departure by five to fifteen minutes.

- Supervise students as they move through the hallways.

- Discuss potential situations with your students and have them devise various ways of avoiding problems.

- If you are on recess supervision, be outside immediately. If necessary, have a teacher in a nearby classroom dismiss your students.

- Ensure that students do not bring expensive personal items or significant sums of money into the school environment. The presence of these items is an invitation for theft and extortion.

- Provide sufficient equipment at recess to ensure that students have lots of activities to keep them busy.

- Employ security cameras to monitor areas of the school that are frequently hidden from view. Similarly, consider installing cameras in school buses to avoid unsafe situations.

- For young children who cannot sit on the floor in a group situation, provide them with a chair or have them sit immediately next to you, before problems develop.

- Stop unsafe situations before they occur. You do not have to wait until a student throws something at another student. Intervene according to your professional judgment.

- Work with school bus drivers to ensure that serious problems do not occur on the way to school. These problems usually carry over into the school environment.

CHAPTER
NINETEEN

Set High Standards

# Set High Standards

Consider this everyday classroom scenario in which the teacher uses a management strategy to encourage a student to complete an assignment. Joey submits his assignment to the teacher who quickly realizes that it is very poorly done. She calls him up to her desk and says, "Joey, this assignment you just turned in is disorganized and incomplete. If you turn it in this way, you will get an F." What do you think his response will be? "Okay. I'll take it back and redo it." "How much more would I have to do to get a passing grade?" "I don't care. Give it an F if you want to." The teacher, of course, hopes he will decide against getting an F, take the work back, and complete it. However, the choice is his. This is an "If ... then ..." statement. It is a choice, not a limit. What it actually communicates to the student is, "Joey, if you don't mind getting an F, then you have my permission to turn in your assignment disorganized and incomplete."

In effect, behavior management gives students the option of underachieving if they are willing to live with low marks. Unfortunately, many students could not care less about marks. This entire scenario violates one of the most basic ethical principles of the education profession, our guarantee as professional educators that we will require students to work up to their level of capability, that underachievement is not a student choice. Ensuring that students do not underachieve is an adult responsibility and is one of the most basic building blocks in the teacher-parent partnership ... and we gave it away!

When students do not care about their marks and about the quality of their work, it is up to the teacher to care. That is a teacher's job—to care about standards until students care and are ready to take them over. The person who cares is the person who makes the decision.

So, when a student tries to submit work that is below standards, use discipline rather than management. Hand it right back and say, "I'm not accepting this. You can do better. Take it back and do it again. I'm not marking it at all until it's done properly."

Then apply this concept to all student behavior. Do not accept underachievement in any form. Send the student back to do it again. This concept also applies to the way they speak to you or to other students, how they handle frustration and anger, how they deal with substitute teachers—everything. Remember, real discipline gives the message that the only way you will behave is the right way, so get used to it.

**Get Your Money's Worth**

Instead of accepting whatever the students give you and simply encouraging them to do more, be demanding. All good teachers are. They challenge students, push students, and whatever else it takes to get them to work up to their potential. Look at it this way. It costs approximately 35 dollars a day for a student to go to school, whether they attend or not. Double that for most special education students and triple it for those in very special programs where extra staff is required, including behavioral programs. That is a lot of money, so make sure you get your money's worth every single day.

After all, you would expect a plumber to finish the job you are paying him to do, wouldn't you? Would you let a roofer only do half your roof after you paid him to do your entire roof? Then, make sure students get the message as well. At the end of the day, ask them what they learned, whom they helped, and what they contributed. Insist that they complete assigned tasks and solve any problems that arise during the course of the day. If they cannot respond appropriately, the day is not over.

Make them understand the importance of good attendance. The money is being spent even if they are not at school. People want a good return on their investment, and they are not getting it if students are wandering the streets instead of in school.

**Keep Raising the Bar**

When you teach mathematics, you consistently raise your expectations. As soon as the students know a skill, you move on to a more difficult one. You keep reviewing any skills you already covered, of course, but you also keep adding new ones. In addition, you work with other teachers, building on each other's efforts, thereby creating a powerful effect called continuous progress or continuous growth. By the very structure of education, students are required to improve their skills as they go through school, an intuitive concept for you as an educator. That is why, if you were given a series of mathematics questions from different grade levels, you could quickly match them. Try it. Here are four questions drawn from grades one, three, five, and eight. Quickly match them.

| **A** | **B** | **C** | **D** |
|---|---|---|---|
| $93 \times 18 =$ | $2 + 1 =$ | $(47 \times 39) / 16 + 24 =$ | $26 / 88 =$ |

Easy, wasn't it? As an educator, you know how the system works. (Okay, the answers are B-D-A-C, as if you did not know.) You also know this effect is not reversible. If a student entered grade one able to do the difficult question in square C, and by grade eight could only answer two plus one, you would be concerned about the possibility of a serious health problem. How else could the student go backward in his learning? If this problem is so obvious, then what has happened to our behavioral expectations for our children? *Behavior is now the only major area of child development where we actually tolerate deterioration over time.*

We rationalize this deterioration with a series of excuses like, "Kids will be kids." "The hormones are running." "Look at the homes they come from." The fact is that hormones and poor home situations affect mathematics as well, along with every other subject in school. But we change our teaching techniques, not our expectations. So, let's go back to expecting the students in grade two to behave one year better than they did in grade one. Then, let's teach them to do so. If we carry this concept all the way up through all the grades, the oldest students will be the best-behaved students in the school.

Don't think it is possible? Take a good look at your students. Eighty percent of them already meet this expectation, the reason why we have so many great adolescents in the world today. It is the other twenty percent who make everyone look bad. Behavior management gave them the option of deteriorating as long as they were willing to live with the consequences of their actions. Underachievement was never intended to be a child choice, whether in academics or behavior.

## Be Clear and Consistent

It is not enough to simply have high standards. They must also be visible to other people, particularly parents, and they need to be consistent. You will understand why these visible standards are important when you understand the impact of human nature. People draw conclusions that are based on what they can see, and make assumptions about what they cannot see. If you are buying a new car and there are flaws in the paint job, you immediately question the integrity of other components in the car. Maybe the engine is shoddily built as well! When food stores put their house brands of cereal in cheap, one-color boxes, consumers quickly adopt the belief that the cereal is also cheap, despite the fact that it is made by the major manufacturers. Hence, if you allow students to take work home when it is still full of errors, parents look at the work and draw conclusions about everything else that goes on at school throughout the day. A number of years ago, for example, teachers were into "inventive spelling." Parents looked at this schoolwork, which was full of "errors," and immediately became concerned about the quality of everything else that was occurring in the schools.

Hence, your standards need to be evident in everything you do, from student assignments and marking systems to student behavior and personal professionalism. If you have a mix of high standards and low standards, then you have low standards. To maintain high standerds, you can do the following:

- On the first day of school, have students do one assignment carefully and neatly. Put this assignment up on a bulletin board or insert it in the student's portfolio and use the work as your ongoing comparison for quality standards. The rest of the student's work should be at least as good as the sample.

- Use bulletin boards to display examples of high-quality work.

- Make sure that work sent home to parents is high quality—if not, then stamp it "draft" or "work in progress."

- Require students to behave in a way that meets your overall standards. The behavior of students makes a significant impact on the impressions that parents hold about schools. You cannot be a high-standards school if student behavior is low quality.

- Inform parents about standards right at the start of the school year. If you are going to require students to redo messy assignments, then parents should know why. Otherwise, they could interpret your actions as "picky" and unreasonable.

- Make sure your classroom is well organized and neatly decorated. You lose your credibility when you demand neat, well-organized assignments at the same time that you model disorganization and lack of commitment.

- Recognize that your own appearance and conduct as a professional reflects on everything else you do. A casual appearance suggests casual standards. Many teachers claim that their clothing should not matter since it is their skills that count. Obviously, skills are very important. However, when people get on airplanes, most of them genuinely appreciate seeing the pilots dressed in immaculate uniforms. If the pilots were dressed in dirty t-shirts and ripped cut-off jeans, their skills would be exactly the same, but the confidence that people have in their skills would not be. So, present yourself in a way that inspires confidence.

- Take another lesson from the airlines. When you fly, have you noticed how the cabin staff clean up before the plane lands? During the last five minutes, they go through the plane and collect garbage, headsets, newspapers, etc. Try doing the same thing in your classroom at the end of the day. It is a matter of respect for the environment and also for the cleaning staff who are hired to clean, not to tidy up.

CHAPTER TWENTY

# Treat Parents as Partners

# Treat Parents as Partners

*For the past twenty years, parents and teachers have been employing behavior management techniques. Hence, for the past twenty years, parents and teachers have focused on incidents and their responses to those incidents.*

- Parents bring their children to school and tell the teachers, "If he (or she) does anything wrong, I want to hear about it."

- Teachers write lists of incidents in books and send them home with children, calling these "communication books," when they are actually little more than complaint books.

- Parents come to the school for a formal meeting about their child's behavior. Almost the entire meeting is spent reviewing the child's involvement in incidents and deciding what will be done in response to the next incident.

- Frustrated parents begin to blame teachers, claiming that teachers get paid to deal with incidents that occur at school.

- Frustrated teachers begin to blame parents, claiming that parents are not being supportive because they are not following through in regard to incidents that occur at school.

This is not the way it is supposed to be. Our preoccupation with incidents and consequences has seriously damaged the positive relationship that should exist between parents and teachers. We do, after all, share a common objective. We want what is best for the children. Our different viewpoints should be a source of strength, not friction.

Here are some ways to rebuild the relationship:

**Help Parents Refocus**

Parents have come to believe that the best way to support teachers is by focusing on daily incidents. Hence, they make statements such as, "If he does anything wrong, I want to hear about it." Help rebuild the partnership by responding, "No, you don't. I will take care of what happens at school. That is my job. You take care of what happens at home. I promise I will let you know about any serious problems that arise."

## Communication

Parents need to be kept informed about serious incidents and repetitive misbehaviors. This communication should be done in person or on the telephone to permit an open discussion of the issues and the development of a plan of action. Do not report these problems in written notes unless there are no other options.

Communication with a child's parents *does not* involve relating a list of every incident that occurs during school hours. These incidents have already occurred, and it is too late for the parents to do anything constructive about them. All they can do is punish the child, but they are punishing him for behaviors that occurred outside of their jurisdiction and supervision, placing the parents in an impossible position. Although instituting additional punishment would be reactive and of questionable value, any hesitation to do so could be interpreted by the teacher as a lack of support.

True communication elicits support on expectations, not consequences. Focus on how the student should behave in the future, rather than discussing behaviors that are history and cannot be changed. One issue for discussion is the skills that need to be improved: "For the next two weeks, I will be working with Patrick on his courtesy skills, particularly 'please' and 'thank you.' If you have time and can review these behaviors at home, I would appreciate it." This is the same way you would communicate about other aspects of school. For instance, you would request parental assistance in reviewing the multiplication tables. In other words, *give parents something to accomplish, not something to punish.* In addition, you should communicate with parents about procedures that could be used to prevent future problems, rather than consequences for responding to future problems.

## Meetings

A great deal of friction frequently develops when teachers and parents meet to discuss a child's behavioral difficulties. Both sides may feel they are being blamed for the problems and criticized for their inability to find a remedy. Here are some guidelines to ensure that the meeting remains positive and gets the results you desire:

• Adopt a positive attitude. Be pleased—genuinely pleased—that the parents took the time to come in and meet with you.

• Ensure that the parents are treated as partners. Sit around a table instead of playing the power game by sitting behind a desk. Offer the parents a cup of coffee or cool drink to put them at their ease.

• Talk across to parents—not down to them.

• Avoid reviewing a list of incidents. Instead, start by discussing the kind of child you want their child to become. Almost invariably, the parents will agree with you, setting a solid foundation for the rest of the meeting. The most implacable parents are the ones who are half-right. They know they have a valid point to make and will not engage in a productive meeting if their opinions and concerns are ignored. Make sure you acknowledge the points on which parents are correct so they will listen to your view on other issues.

• Develop a plan of action that focuses on how the student will behave appropriately in school, instead of planning adult responses for the next time the child misbehaves (although this could be one small part of the overall plan).

• Remember that parents often know what works with their child. Ask them, and take their opinions into account.

- Respect the demands on the parents' time. A suggestion that parents should quit work in order to supervise their child is inappropriate. Although parents may reach this conclusion themselves, educators should not put themselves in the position of forcing a family into financial distress.

- Express confidence in a child's ability to learn the behavioral lessons that he or she needs to learn. You can never be criticized for believing in the abilities of your students.

- Do not under any circumstances suggest that a particular medical condition is probably at the root of a student's problems.

- Finally, keep in mind that the educational experiences of many parents are negative. Meetings in schools rekindle past memories and may prompt parents to be highly sensitive, defensive, and overreactive. Be understanding. Not everyone perceives the school setting as positive.

## Coordination

- Work with parents to ensure that homework is completed. Communicate work requirements on a daily basis. You may wish to communicate by issuing agenda books to students. If so, take the last five minutes of each day to review information regarding work to be finished along with any tests for which the student should be studying.

- Involve the parents in the development of plans for behavior improvement. Communicate the success of these plans. Ask parents to work with their child at home on the development of desirable behaviors.

- Request parental support in following through on behavioral practice, not punishment, in the home environment.

# Building
# School
# Discipline

CHAPTER
TWENTY
ONE

# Rebuild Teamwork

# Rebuild Teamwork

*Effective school discipline requires teamwork.*
*Only when teachers work together are they able to achieve the consistency*
*necessary to create a positive school culture and teach students*
*how to function within that structure.*

Unfortunately, twenty years of *classroom* management has virtually destroyed the concept of teamwork in today's schools, at least as far as discipline is concerned. At the beginning of the book, we looked at some of the effects created by this extraordinary focus on the classroom. It is very important for everyone to have a clear understanding of what is happening. Hence, let's take another look at those issues and add some additional points:

- Classroom management suggests that discipline is a matter of what individual teachers do in their own classrooms with their own students. As a result, we now have many schools where all teachers do their own thing concerning discipline, including setting their own expectations, rules, and consequences.

- Teachers come to believe that the way their students behave in other classrooms is solely the responsibility of the teachers in those rooms. Hence, they only deal with their own students in the hallways, lunchrooms, and other common areas.

- Teachers perceive supervision outside of the classroom as an extra chore rather than as an integral part of discipline. They believe it is to be avoided unless it is mandated under the supervision schedule.

- The lack of consistency across the school environment takes away the parental sense of what the school, as a whole, expects. Instead, they have to deal with the different expectations of each teacher. As a result, parents are highly likely to challenge the beliefs of individual teachers and claim that certain teachers are unfair.

- Teachers lose the concept of building on top of what the previous teacher accomplished. They also do not systematically prepare the children for future grades.

- Since teachers no longer speak with one voice, schools have lost the part of school culture that blocks students from bringing their home and community behaviors into the school environment. As a result, students now display the same behaviors in school as they do outside of school.

### Struggling to Get Our Act Together

I hope that you now understand the full impact of classroom management on discipline in our schools and on the sense of teamwork among teachers. However, let's be absolutely clear on just how far it has gone. We have now reached the point where many school staffs cannot even get teamwork on something as simple as the enforcement of a "no gum-chewing" rule. Even when such a rule is supposed to be schoolwide, there are frequently one or two teachers on a staff who will attempt to gain favoritism with their own students by allowing them to break the rule.

Teachers who permit this behavior usually argue that gum chewing is a minor issue and there are more important things worthy of concern. In fact, gum chewing is not the issue at all. The issue is whether or not teachers understand how to work as members of a professional, collegial team. The difference becomes clear on closer examination of the issue. When gum chewing is disallowed across a school environment, it is because the staff made a decision to eliminate this nuisance behavior by consistently enforcing a ban. This decision was approved by the principal and written into the school rules. Then, one or two teachers arbitrarily decide to do their own thing and allow their own students to chew gum. By doing so, they ensure that a behavior which was supposed to be a non-issue throughout the school is now going to be an issue in everyone's classroom but theirs, thereby deliberately sabotaging the efforts of their colleagues. In addition, they model for the students in their classes deliberate defiance of school rules and overt disrespect for authority. The issue is not gum chewing; it is unprofessional conduct.

What some teachers fail to realize these days is that being a member of a team means you do not get your own way all the time. You have to learn to work within a team structure and to recognize that an individual is designated as being in charge of the team. Your job is to implement the decisions that are made, not ignore them. When teachers realize what it means to be a member of a team, they realize that their personal preferences do not supersede their professional responsibilities.

This message may strike some teachers as unduly blunt. Unfortunately, it is essential that the point be made. After all, how will we ever get on top of bullying and violence if we cannot get our acts together on chewing gum, leaving hats off, walking in the hallways, and not littering? With that having been said, it is time to make a personal decision. *Are you a classroom teacher or a school teacher?*

Decide now, because there is a very big difference between the two. Of course, if your position does not quite fit this query, then substitute your title in the place of *classroom teacher*. Whether you are a resource teacher, physics teacher, or special education teacher, the question remains the same.

For discipline to work in a school, you must adopt the following belief: "Together, we are the teachers of all of the students at our school." It is true, of course, that all teachers have a primary area of responsibility. Certain students are directly under their tutelage. However, there is also a bigger picture. Unless each teacher subscribes to this bigger picture, schoolwide discipline cannot be implemented.

Keep in mind that everyone in the learning community is part of the team, including secretaries, teaching assistants, caretakers, and other personnel. (School secretaries are often the best disciplinarians in the school. They do not let students get away with anything. Students cannot even hand in the attendance folder the wrong way.)

Keep in mind that the mere act of assigning an educational assistant to deal with a child's behavioral difficulties adds to the unfortunate perception that specific individuals are responsible for student behavior in the school environment.

To be a team member, here are some of the things that you must be willing to do:

- Be willing to put aside some personal preferences in favor of implementing and enforcing group decisions.

- Be prepared to put up with some personal inconvenience if decisions are made regarding professional appearance and apparel.

- Be prepared to attend additional in-service sessions that will likely be required in order to coordinate staff beliefs and make group decisions regarding rules and procedures. There is a high probability that these meetings would have to be scheduled during teacher breaks in order to implement effective discipline immediately when students return from their holidays.

- Be willing to deal with other teachers' students, to support colleagues, and to share the load.

- Be willing to look at your beliefs regarding discipline, a process that may cause some discomfort.

- If you are authoritarian in your teaching style, it will be necessary to rely less on the power of consequences and to commit the time required to develop true authority.

- Be willing to work on building a partnership with parents.

CHAPTER
TWENTY
TWO

# Get Everyone on the Same Page,
# Going in the Same Direction

# Get Everyone on the Same Page, Going in the Same Direction

*Once a sense of teamwork has been established,
the next step is to develop shared concepts
regarding expectations, goals, and rules.*

## Common Beliefs

Start by sharing beliefs about discipline. It is essential for everyone to develop a positive view of discipline. Otherwise, strategies will not be implemented consistently, some teachers will continue to rely heavily on consequences, and some teachers will undermine the school's initiative. Attempt to get all teachers to perceive discipline as primarily preventative in nature. Help them understand the critical nature of supervision and authority.

Develop a common language in regard to discipline and student behavior. For instance, discuss issues such as extensions and detentions, which are very different concepts. (When a student stays after school to practice desired behavior, it is not a detention because there is no punishment. It is an extension—the student must stay late because his work is not finished.)

## Vision

Then, decide together what it means to be a student of your school. Develop a picture of how the students look, talk, walk, and work.

Take a look at the list of questions on pages 86 and 87. Use them to help guide staff discussions. You should be able to reach a consensus. Keep in mind, however, that consensus does not mean decisions must be unanimous. As long as there is a consensus, teachers who disagree should be prepared to abide by the group's decision.

One of the most important decisions to be made is whether your school will become a learning community where students act and dress in accordance with high standards and expectations—or will it be an extension of the students' home environments? There is a big difference! If you want a learning community, you must be prepared to establish a clear threshold and ensure that teachers consistently reject unacceptable behaviors—"Not here!" Decide on a number of ways to differentiate the school environment from the home and community environments. Start with simple rules such as "hats off." Then consider the value of a more extensive dress code. Most schools refuse to allow short-shorts, halter tops, belly shirts, droopy and baggy pants, gang paraphernalia, and excessive body piercing. Other schools go so far as to require students to wear a school uniform, or school clothing that is provided in a variety of mix and match styles and colors. This type of clothing makes students look like they come from a high-standards school. They appear self-disciplined, well organized, and respectful.

If you want a school with high standards, everything must give that message. Consistency, after all, is an issue of expectations and how the expectations are communicated and enforced. Hence, teachers should be prepared to abide by a dress code as well.

Like it or not, casual clothing denotes casual standards. Also, think back to the example given in chapter 19. When you get on an airplane, chances are that you appreciate the pilot being dressed in an immaculate uniform. Although the pilot's skills would be exactly the same if he were dressed in a dirty t-shirt and shorts, your confidence in his skills would not be. You would be seriously concerned about his level of commitment. This is exactly how parents feel when they see teachers dressed casually.

Note that many schools are moving away from the traditional professional dress because of the extraordinary discomfort that results in non-air-conditioned schools. Instead, the schools are developing their own lines of clothing. For instance, they may provide well-tailored "golf" shirts emblazoned with the school crest and name, as well as the word *Staff.* These shirts are produced in the school colors, thereby allowing teachers to be professional and comfortable at the same time. The color coordination also makes the staff appear to be a team.

One other area that should not be overlooked when it comes to the communication of high standards is the school building itself and the grounds surrounding it. It is important for these to be well maintained. Understand that a school with litter all over its grounds does not look like a school with high standards.

### Structure

Once all staff members have a common vision, then work on the development of consistent rules, limits, and procedures that will apply to all common areas throughout the school. Also, consider common expectations for classrooms such as "Be on time" and "Complete your assignments."

### Skills

Should certain skills be taught to all students in the school? What about courtesy? Is there a need to teach students how to treat substitute teachers? Should the physical education teacher be spending the first couple of weeks teaching playground games so students will know the rules and be able to organize their own activities?

Coordinate staff efforts when teaching behavioral skills. Their efforts will show greater results if key skills are taught at the same time in all classrooms. To this end, many schools focus on a "skill-a-month," emphasizing the skill through teacher-directed practice, morning announcements, classroom storytelling, and the production of signs and bulletin boards.

Develop recognition programs that may be used to show students that their efforts have been noticed and are appreciated. Allow students to enter their names in drawings, with the tickets being given out by teachers in response to positive behavior. Commend great behavior during the morning announcements. Mount student pictures on bulletin boards. (Note that these rewards are being used to *support* discipline, not to *replace* discipline.)

### The Importance of Leadership

Leadership is a critical factor in the development of school discipline. The principal of a school must be prepared to take charge of the process and ensure that all people and elements come together. In addition, the principal must be willing to deal with reluctant teachers. The principal's responsibilities include the following tasks:

- Build common beliefs, language, and expectations based on a positive view of discipline.

- Create an atmosphere in which teachers can freely express ideas, concerns, and dissenting opinions.

- Build a sense of teamwork by dealing effectively with teachers who want to "do their own thing."

- Facilitate an open exchange of information.

- Keep parents onside.

- Ensure that effective supervision is implemented.

- Support the supervision process through personal presence in all common areas.

- Support the development of positive teacher authority.

- Arrange meetings and schedules to ensure that sufficient time is dedicated to the development phase.

- Ensure that staff follows through with decisions and commitments.

- Create mechanisms for ongoing evaluation and review of the school discipline process.

### What About Kids' Rights?

These days, many teachers get hung up on the issue of kids' rights. They become concerned during discussions about rules that forbid students to wear their hats in school, chew gum, wear t-shirts with violent images, or show their belly buttons. Their concern is that these rules violate the rights of students. Many parents also become very agitated when they are told that their children are not allowed to dress a certain way, particularly parents who generally allow their children to "do their own thing" as a means of keeping the peace at home. These parents are often very quick to rescue their children whenever there is a conflict at school.

In fact, there is really no need for a prolonged debate on this issue. It is simply time to recognize that *having the right to do something does not make it the right thing to do.* The law deals with the issue of personal rights and freedoms. Discipline teaches students to do what is right according to the demands of the situation. A business executive has the right to go to work wearing pajamas. However, to do so would be wrong because it would be inappropriate. Schools are trying to deal with this issue of inappropriateness. Although technically students have the legal right to wear their hats in school, wearing hats is inappropriate within a learning environment. So, instead of focusing on the issue of kids' rights, let's concentrate on teaching students to do what is right.

CHAPTER
TWENTY
THREE

# Work Together to Make it Happen

# Work Together
# to Make It Happen

*To achieve an effective level of discipline throughout the school environment,
it is essential for teachers to coordinate their efforts,
support their colleagues, and create joint problem-solving solutions.*

Here are a few of the many ways to work together:

- Coordinate a schoolwide training camp.

- Correct any student, anywhere, anytime.

- If you have older students, think about how they can be of assistance to younger students. Offer this help to the teachers of the younger students.

- When your students are on rotary, work with the rotary teacher to ensure quality behavior.

- Spontaneously provide extra supervision when it is necessary, even if it is not your turn.

- Be willing to cover for each other when dealing with particularly difficult students. If teachers share responsibilities for the most difficult students, no one will become totally worn out or stressed out. (See Chapter 29 for additional details.)

- If you know a substitute teacher will be coming in, offer to take a difficult student from that room for the day.

- Coordinate the teaching of specific skills.

- Deal with the behavior of all students, not just your own. (Do not threaten punishment. Just be assertive.)

- Provide the mutual support and sharing of tasks that would naturally occur if you were team-teaching in the same room.

- Offer to have a younger student sit next to an older student in your classroom if it would help the younger student complete his work.

- Work in partnership with parents as well. Communicate with them about what you are trying to accomplish with their child and ask them to work on the same behaviors and attitudes at home, the real meaning of parental support.

## Require Growth Across the Grades

Students are supposed to improve as they get older. They improve in mathematics, reading, sports, computers, video games—everything except behavior. With behavior, a significant number of students deteriorate over the years because management techniques allow students to make this choice, provided they are willing to accept the consequences of their actions.

To avoid this problem, each teacher should build on the work of the previous teacher. In addition, the teacher should have a clear concept of what is required for success in the upcoming year. Communication and planning are necessary. Following is a chart that shows the building of compliance skills across the grades. The skills are cumulative. Hence, the skill listed for grade 3 is to be added to all previous items. In Appendix B, you will find a series of charts that will assist you in developing a scope and sequence for behavior improvement across the grades. These charts were designed by groups of regular class teachers at each grade level and are intended to show how students would progress if teachers required them to behave one year better in each successive grade. As you will see, student behavior improves dramatically.

# Compliance (Respect for Rules)

### Kindergarten
Learn classroom routines
Follow teacher directions

### Grade 1
Follow rules for playground, recess, and lunch
Require fewer adults on trips
Comply with teacher designates

### Grade 2
Comply with and assist teacher designates

### Grade 3
Comply with students who are designated as group leaders

### Grade 4
Comply despite negative peer pressure

### Grade 5
Comply for the right reasons
Understand rationale for rules

### Grade 6
Are expected to serve as models for younger students
Reach consensus through discussion
Take ownership
Suggest extra rules

### Grades 7 and 8
Differentiate between positive and negative leadership
Adjust to new school situation and new peers (where appropriate)
Comply without excessive supervision
Handle rules applied flexibly

## Discipline is a Process, Not an Event

The implementation of effective school discipline is a task that never ends. Revisions and improvements must constantly be made in response to changes in student behaviors and needs. Therefore, it is essential for teachers to approach discipline as an ongoing process.

Meet regularly to review progress toward specific goals, evaluate problems that may have arisen, and recommend refinements that may be required. Establish a committee to gather data and make it available to staff in a condensed format. Doing so saves a considerable amount of time and energy.

# Applications

CHAPTER
TWENTY
FOUR

# Problem Solving

# Problem Solving

Throughout this book, you have been asked to examine your beliefs. It is important to see discipline positively, to believe it is about teaching students to be responsible and cooperative. If you hold this view, it will affect everything you do including the problem solving that is required for dealing with difficult cases.

When management techniques are employed, problem solving generally involves an analysis of incidents, the use of guidance to convince students to avoid any repetition of these incidents, and the application of stiffer consequences, should such repetition occur. Discipline, on the other hand, relies mostly on prevention. The goal of any problem solving is to decide how the student will behave appropriately in the future.

Plan for how students will behave well, not what you will do when they do not.

Here are some questions to help you with your line of reasoning:

- How can the structure be changed to prevent incidents?

- What changes need to be made in terms of supervision?

- If the student is noncompliant, how can effective training be accomplished to decrease the number of confrontations?

- Since compliance must be trained on small behaviors, what is the present situation regarding the enforcement of minor directions, rules, and procedures? What changes need to be made?

- How do we want this student to behave by the end of this week, month, term, or year? What skills will he have to learn in order to accomplish this goal? How will he be taught these skills?

- Are the parents able to support the school's efforts? If so, how will a partnership be built with them? How will they be enlisted to practice the desired behaviors in the home environment? (Remember to give parents something to accomplish, not something to punish.)

In the following chapters, these questions are consistently employed in determining effective strategies for dealing with specific problems. For instance, in considering how to deal with impulsive children at recess time, it is recommended that these children be required to plan their recess activities before leaving the classroom. Advance planning is the opposite of impulsivity. Discipline is not about waiting for incidents to occur and then responding. It is about making sure the incidents do not happen in the first place.

### Remember

Discipline is determined mainly by insights, not
incidents. When you know that a student is likely to have
a problem, intervene so he will not.

CHAPTER TWENTY FIVE

# Dealing With ADD and ADHD

# Dealing With ADD and ADHD

The number of children diagnosed as having Attention Deficit Disorder (ADD) has risen substantially over the past decade. Since ADD has a significant impact on the functioning of children within the school environment, teachers need practical interventions for dealing with their behavioral difficulties.

ADD is generally considered to be related to the metabolic levels in the parts of the brain that deal with attention and self-control. These levels are lower than normal and dwindle quickly when the individual is confronted with mundane tasks, creating the attentional difficulties typically shown by ADD students. The problem, however, is not that ADD students cannot pay attention; it is that they pay attention to everything. They particularly pay attention to things that are more interesting than what they are supposed to be doing.

In addition, there tends to be a slow transmission of messages across the synapses of the central nervous system. It takes an unusually long time for these individuals to think through information, especially in complex social problem-solving situations, such as playground activities. This need for extensive time to think through information creates the impulsive behaviors typical of ADD students. Quite literally, they act before they complete the thinking process.

With Attention Deficit Hyperactivity Disorder (ADHD), there is the addition of hyperactivity that is an excessive level of motor movement. Hyperactive children are always in motion. It is believed that this outward motion usually compensates for the sluggishness within the body's systems. Remember that the same behavior patterns can be caused by other factors. For instance, children who live in chaos with no structure or routines may develop a behavior pattern known as "agitation." Agitation mimics ADD and ADHD. In addition, spirited children are often mislabeled as being ADD, along with some gifted children.

ADD is a true disorder (in that it makes the individual dysfunctional) for about ten percent of the individuals who receive the diagnosis. For the majority, it is best perceived as a set of traits, albeit an *annoying* set of traits.

The most common medical intervention is the administration of a mild stimulant, usually Ritalin (Methylphenidate Hydrochloride). The drug is believed to increase the metabolic rate in the sluggish portions of the brain, thereby improving attentional abilities. It also increases the speed of message transmission across the central nervous system, thereby decreasing impulsivity.

### Strategies Related to Attention

- Have the student repeat your directions.

- Announce what you are going to say before you say it.

- Provide the student with a quiet place to work in addition to a regular desk.

- "Chunk" the student's work and provide frequent changes.

- Have the student work with a non-ADD student (but not the same student all the time).

- Make frequent eye contact.

- Keep the student busy but provide breaks.

- Seat the child near your desk or close to where you spend most of your time.

- Use extra motivation but think in terms of challenges, not bribes.

- Monitor progress often. The student needs frequent feedback.

- Teach outlining, underlining, and organizational skills.

### Strategies Related to Impulsivity

- Provide structure, rules, routines, and direction. ADD students are at risk whenever they are required to think for themselves. Because their thinking processes are so slow, their behaviors will instead be based on impulsivity, and they will get into trouble many, many times, often repeating the same errors. Hence, these students need to be relieved of the need to apply their own thinking. Instead, their actions should be governed by structure, rules, routines, and adult direction.

- Since preplanning is the opposite of impulsivity, help them think through a situation and plan their actions ahead of time. For instance, before going out onto the playground, ADD students should be required to tell the teacher what games they are going to play, with whom, where, and who has the equipment.

- Help students make their own schedules for after school. Consider providing them with organizers. Schedule a time each day for having the organizers completed.

- Create some escape valves that allow students to escape difficult situations, possibly by leaving the class for a moment. Teach the students how and when to use these outlets.

- Provide feedback to help these children become more observant of their own behavior.

- Provide social coaching to help them deal with situations that could provoke problems.

- Prepare these children for unstructured times.

- Pre-teach desired behaviors.

- Since handwriting is very difficult for some of these students, consider alternatives, particularly keyboarding.

- With older children, stress preparation prior to coming to class.

- Provide extra supervision.

- Train automatic behaviors and compliance. Impulsivity tends to govern thinking behaviors (because it is defined as acting before the completion of the thinking process). Therefore, the more these students can work from the nonthinking part of the brain, the fewer problems they have.

• Use instruction, tell them what to do, have them repeat instructions, and reinforce correct responses.

# CHAPTER TWENTY SIX

# Dealing With
# Disruptive Students

# Dealing With
# Disruptive Students

In today's schools, teachers are faced with extraordinary curriculum demands. To be successful, teachers must be able to minimize any disruption within the classroom. In fact, virtually every study of effective schools confirms that effective teachers protect the integrity of the learning environment. The following will assist you in protecting the integrity of your learning environment by minimizing disruptions:

- Examine your seating arrangements. If you have arranged student desks in a manner that stimulates conversation and interaction (such as in groups), then your classroom design is part of the problem.

- Continue your lesson while moving toward the attention-seeking student, using your physical proximity to subdue the behavior. Attention seeking is the one behavior that responds positively to being ignored.

- When dealing with interruptions, consider the age of the children. Young children interrupt because whatever is on their mind is the most important issue in the world at that moment. They are absolutely convinced that you must be just as concerned about it as they are. At this age, they must be taught when interruptions are appropriate and when they are considered rude.

- For older children who should know better, respond with a signal such as holding out your hand in a typical "stop" motion. However, do not respond either with your voice or your eyes. The latter part is particularly difficult and must be practiced. It is important because, in our culture, we use both our voices and our eyes to start conversations. If you turn and speak to children when they interrupt, they will start to say whatever is on their mind. But if you turn and make eye contact with them, that starts them talking as well. A "stop" hand signal is the most effective response. Then, at the right time, remember to ask them what they wanted to say.

• For students who throw objects around the room, take all potential objects from them, including anything that may be in their desks. Use physical proximity and supervision to limit the ability of students to engage in such behavior.

• Investigate whether or not a student is capable of doing work. When a student wanders around the classroom, work avoidance is one of the possible causes. Make adjustments if necessary. Redirect the student to his desk. Some students need to move around every so often, especially those who are diagnosed as ADD or ADHD. These students should be provided with opportunities to have their needs met in nondisruptive ways. Let them move back and forth between two desks. Provide an area where they can stand and work. Occasionally send them to the office with messages, thereby giving them a physical break.

• If a student enjoys bothering others, move that student's desk to a location close to where you spend most of your time. If necessary, use isolation. Ensure that you have the student practice skills for sitting quietly and respecting the rights of others.

• Teach students how to choose the right time and place for inserting humorous comments, how to respond positively to signals from you, and how to judge the appropriateness of comments. Some students love to play the role of class clown. Often, such students will truly have a great sense of humor.

CHAPTER
TWENTY
SEVEN

# Dealing With
# Aggression and Violence

# Dealing With Aggression and Violence

For some students, physical aggression presents an extraordinarily effective means of controlling the environment and meeting personal needs. Frequently, students disregard school rules that prohibit this behavior in favor of their personal view that aggression is a legitimate way of protecting their rights and interests. This view often receives active support within the home environment and community as well as the students' peer groups. Students who are oriented toward the use of aggression may focus on media presentations that validate this perspective. All this support allows aggressive students to maintain high self-esteem, contrary to the popular notion that aggressive students must have low self-esteem.

As a staff, address the need to deal with contributing behaviors including put-downs, aggressive teasing, and general disrespect. These behaviors frequently escalate into physical confrontations and aggression. Do not overlook "small" incidents—students interpret lack of teacher intervention as tacit permission.

For students who consistently bully others, restructure their school day to eliminate the opportunities for aggression. Upon their arrival at school, they should be escorted into the building and supervised from that moment on. Do not permit them out onto school grounds without direct supervision. Provide an alternative recess by allowing them to read, catch up on unfinished work, or work on a computer. (You can provide desirable activities because they have not lost recess. They simply have an alternative recess.) Be particularly careful about structuring and supervising their lunch hour. Also, provide additional structure for washroom visits and end-of-the-day procedures. Stress prevention. Once aggression begins, a situation can quickly spiral out of control. One minute of prevention can save an hour of intervention.

Consequences may be necessary to ensure that students get the message that aggression is forbidden. Remember to use consequences to support your interventions, not to replace your interventions.

Involve parents when students engage in serious or repetitive aggression. Focus on planning for the future. Discussions of past incidents often force parents to defend their children, thereby justifying inappropriate behavior.

When you are called on to break up a fight, resist the temptation to resolve the issues immediately. Emotions are usually much too intense, and the students will simply continue to bicker. Separate them and allow some cooling-off time. It is often possible for the participants to resolve the issues that led to their fight. However, you may need to supervise the discussion to ensure that they know how to problem solve effectively.

Note that most fights begin with verbal "hits." In the future, watch for these and attempt to stop violence at this early level. As verbal sparring begins, consider using the words, "Don't hit." Children are often surprised at this choice of words and will respond, "I didn't touch him." You are then in a position to make the concept of verbal hits clear and to disallow them. It is a much more powerful way of dealing with the issue.

When you break up a fight, deal seriously with any spectators who eagerly supported the conflict. They are involved in the fight just as much as the actual participants. Peer pressure is very important. Spectators should be stopping a fight, not aggravating the situation.

**Violence**

Serious violence in the school environment can quickly destroy years of effort in building positive school culture. When teachers undertake a major initiative aimed at improving discipline across a school, it is essential that they deal with the issue of violence.

Unfortunately, many teachers misidentify violence as being physical aggression alone when, in reality, most violence is verbal, emotional, and psychological. Hence, teachers should not rely on simplistic school rules such as "no body contact." These rules cause teachers to overlook other important issues including put-downs, which are verbal hits. If teachers truly want to stop fights, they must stop put-downs because verbal hits almost invariably precede physical hits. Also note that a "no body contact" rule is senseless in that it presumably disallows holding hands (which is a safety tool on kindergarten trips), playing games of tag, helping another child on a swing by giving him a push, and so on. Teachers will claim that preventing these activities was not the intention. If this is true, then they should say what they really do mean, which is usually "no rough play," etc. To rule out all body contact is equivalent to ruling out teasing. You lose the good with the bad.

To actually say no to violence, every teacher on staff must be prepared to enforce certain rules. If just one staff member declines to do the job, the "no" becomes a "maybe." Working together, the staff ensures that certain behaviors are forbidden, including the following:

- Physical hitting
- Put-downs (including comments regarding someone's family)
- Swearing that is directed at others
- Extortion ("give me your lunch money or else")
- Bullying
- Threats
- Clothing that depicts violent acts or uses violent language
- Violent pictures and stickers on binders
- Playing cards that depict violent scenes
- Art work that depicts "gratuitous" violence **
- Racial slurs
- Sexual harassment and sexual assault
- Weapons or incendiary devices

Make sure that you have school-based solutions for violators of rules involving clothing, binders, and so on. If students are unable to turn the clothing inside out, then they should be able to sign out a "cover-up" at the office. Alternative binders or folders should be available to hold papers that must be removed from unacceptable binders.

\*\*Student Art Work: A school that does not allow violence does not allow students to draw pictures depicting violent scenes, an issue of appropriateness, not an issue of personal expression. Schools would consider pictures of people or animals engaging in sexual coupling to be inappropriate, and violent images fall into the same category. However, there would normally be two exclusions to the rule forbidding violent pictures. One allows students to include historical depictions in specific assignments when authorized by the teacher. The other allows specialized staff to use therapeutic art when they are working with the victims of abuse, violence, or war.

# Dealing with Defiance

# Dealing with Defiance

Almost every teacher will agree that defiance from students is one of the greatest worries in terms of discipline. This behavior is very serious because it directly attacks the authority of the teacher. Unless teachers are able to deal effectively with these types of situations, other students may join in, thereby making it impossible for teachers to do their job. To deal with this behavior, employ the following techniques:

- Lower your voice and become more assertive, not more confrontational. Stay calm. Becoming agitated suggests that the defiant student is winning.

- Do not allow the student to draw you into conflict. Avoid unnecessary confrontation. If necessary, deal with the defiance later.

- Defuse the situation. Humor is often a powerful tool to use in these circumstances.

- Do not challenge a defiant student, particularly in front of his peers, because he would be forced to save face by doing something dramatic. When possible, deal with the student in private.

- Distinguish between "deliberate" defiance and "spontaneous" defiance. Only punish deliberate defiance. Choose a punishment that makes it absolutely clear that this behavior is unacceptable.

- When dealing with defiant students, insist on compliance with minor behaviors such as greetings, saying please and thank you, picking things up, putting things away, and so on. When adults deal with students who engage in serious acts of defiance, there is a very natural tendency—the human nature tendency to "let sleeping dogs lie"—to overlook minor issues in an effort to avoid additional incidents. Unfortunately, this tendency limits the ability of adults to create significant improvement in the behavior of defiant students because compliance must be built by correcting and governing small behaviors.

- Keep in mind that the biggest issue in dealing with an incident is what will be done to ensure that the behavior does not occur again.

- Teach defiant students effective ways of dealing with any frustration or anger that may have precipitated their behavior.

- After an incident, watch for occasions when the student handles similar situations appropriately. Acknowledge the student's efforts in this regard.

CHAPTER
TWENTY
NINE

# Dealing With
# "High-Impact" Students

# Dealing With "High-Impact" Students

"High-impact" students are the ones who have a dramatic, negative effect on the classroom learning environment. These are the students who, if they are absent (which rarely happens), the teacher makes a comment like, "We had a great day because Joey was away sick." This comment sounds unprofessional, because it sounds like the teacher is rejecting the child. Actually, the teacher is rejecting the child's impact on the classroom. When he is there, everybody is under stress. The teacher cannot use humor because she would have to "peel kids off the ceiling." Similarly, the teacher tends to omit high-interest activities and invariably begins to feel that she is failing to provide a high-quality program for the rest of the students who are sitting there waiting to learn. The teacher thus begins a downward spiral that makes the school year very long indeed.

Recognize in this description that the effect does not occur in response to the student's behavior. His mere presence is enough. This effect is rarely recognized by those dealing with child behavior, because management approaches get them to focus on good and bad behavior. When students misbehave, the teacher enforces the consequences. When students behave well, the teacher is supposed to be pleased and reward them ("catch a child being good"). This approach totally misses the fact that children with serious behavior problems are as tiring on their good days as they are on their bad days, because the need for constant vigilance is debilitating. You can never let your guard down. Everyone gets stressed out, including the other students who must constantly be on their guard. When the high-impact student gets out of his seat and walks up the aisle, the other students know that he may do any number of things, such as jabbing someone with a sharp pencil.

High-impact students use their misbehavior to control the world around them. They understand how other people react to them and manipulate those reactions, using their behavior to trigger a predictable sequence of events. They also learn to reverse consequences, manipulate point systems, and discourage adults from putting demands on them. They have a very powerful and successful behavior pattern. It works, at least in the short term.

Here are some suggestions for working with these students:

- Resist the temptation to offer bigger and bigger rewards in an effort to convince these students that cooperation is worthwhile. This type of program feeds their selfish attitudes. The students will happily go along with it, playing you to see how much they can get while simultaneously giving less and less. Never try to out-manipulate manipulators. You will lose.

- Focus on preventative and proactive strategies. Predictable, reactive systems make these kids stronger, not weaker.

- Apply higher levels of supervision, not because they deserve it but because they need it.

- Teach small behaviors, including courtesy skills and entry routines, which are almost invariably ignored for behavioral kids. As a result, they have few routines or habits, especially compliance. It is impossible to create a positive behavior pattern in these students if teachers only respond to major incidents.

- Restructure to ensure that the student's behavior and presence do not produce unwarranted levels of stress for others in a classroom and do not interfere unduly with the teacher's ability to provide appropriate learning for other students in the class. Consider creating an alternative timetable that removes the high-impact student from the classroom for blocks of time. This removal is predetermined and is noncontingent (not determined by the student's behavior). In elementary school, remove the student for approximately twenty-five minutes in the middle of each quarter of the day. During this time, he engages in appropriate educational activities in an alternative location. These activities include the completion of work assigned in the classroom, direct assistance from the learning resource teacher, counseling, peer tutoring, reading buddies, computers, and special research or service projects.

- If rewards are used, ensure that they are "shared" rewards so everyone benefits from good behavior. After all, everyone loses as a result of misbehavior. Shared rewards also improve a difficult student's status in his peer group.

- Insist that difficult students do things for others, including the community at large. These students tend to be extraordinarily self-centered and selfish. It is very important for them to be involved in "service" projects, both big and small.

- Create opportunities for difficult students to work with young children. They often display excellent behavior when they are engaged in these activities.

- Pay special attention to the need to identify a potentially great skill in each student and design opportunities to develop this skill. Research indicates that difficult students only make successful transitions to positive behavior if they have something on which to "hang their egos." Unless their pride comes from skills that we develop in them, it will come from association with a particular group. Be creative. There are many examples of boys being proud of their skills in singing, ballet, and even needlepoint. Girls may likewise be proud of sports, debating, or mechanics.

## "Ganging Up"

When there are several difficult students in one classroom, they quickly learn to "gang up" on the teacher by becoming mutually supportive of each other's misbehavior. The moment any one of them misbehaves, the others begin to make supportive comments, engage in similar behaviors, and escalate the pattern until the teacher's lesson is destroyed.

When "ganging up" occurs, it is important for the teacher to make structural changes that interfere with the problem. Separate the students physically. Meet with them individually before or after school and develop specific plans for handling various classroom situations. Require them to practice appropriate behaviors.

If necessary, and it often is, vary the programming for the students so that one or two of them are out of the classroom during critical time periods. This action stops the interactions that would otherwise interfere with the lesson. Ensure that they are doing suitable educational work. Also, do any restructuring noncontingently so that the changes are not done in response to incidents. Instead, the changes are made to prevent incidents. You do not want to allow students to use their misbehavior to trigger a predictable sequence of events.

### Specialized Behavioral Programs

Many school districts provide specialized behavioral programs that are intended to deal with very difficult students who cannot be successfully maintained in a regular school environment. These special programs are usually segregated (congregated) in design, maintaining the difficult students in a separate classroom while significantly limiting inclusion opportunities. In addition, many districts are experimenting with other models in which students are either partially or fully integrated into mainstream classes and receiving specialized support. Each model has significant advantages and disadvantages when compared to other models.

Be very careful when clustering behavioral students together. Putting eight adolescents with severe behavior problems in the same room is called a "gang," not a class. The program was supposed to be designed to prevent this problem, not encourage it.

Another serious problem with many behavioral programs is that staff may inadvertently be drawn into doing more of what did not work in the first place. They use bigger reward programs and bigger deals. Students may be required to earn the very things that make school worthwhile—physical education, computers, extracurricular activities, excursions, and so on. There is also a tendency to individualize the programs in a way that increases a student's self-centeredness and selfishness.

Behavioral programs should be perceived as "discipline immersion." The purpose is not to provide more intensive management, but rather to provide the intensive training and teaching that the student did not receive in the past. Physical education and computers should be noncontingent, because the purpose of the program is to provide the students with what they *need,* not with what they *deserve.*

# CHAPTER THIRTY

## Potpourri

# Potpourri

## Homework

Everyone knows that homework is important. After all, it is clearly impossible for children to prepare themselves for the modern world in just five hours each school day. Unfortunately, getting students to complete their homework can be a very frustrating task.

To deal with the issue, let's first establish the roles. When teachers assign work, it is their job to check for accuracy and completion. Parents are responsible for creating a structure in the home environment that promotes the completion of homework. Students need an appropriate work location, supervision, and assistance as required.

Both individual teachers and school staffs as a whole should decide what priority is to be placed on homework completion. If it is a high priority, then teachers must be prepared to invest time and energy in providing a structure that sets children up for success and that motivates them to achieve their goals. The only real question should be *when* homework will be completed, *not whether*. It is important for this perspective to be instilled in students right from the primary grades.

Children do not arrive at school naturally endowed with homework abilities. Homework involves skills that must be taught, practiced, and consistently monitored. Remember that students who tend to be disorganized, slow, off task, and irresponsible at school are bound to display identical behaviors at home. Realistically, parents are only able to assist with monitoring if the teacher provides them with a detailed homework communication book. Set aside a few minutes of school time each day for the completion of this book. Teach students how to use the books efficiently and consistently.

Recognizing that many students work better at school than at home, most secondary schools and all universities provide students with the opportunity to stay after classes and work in certain classrooms, the library, or a study hall. Elementary schools could do likewise, with teachers supervising on a rotating basis. Additionally, secondary school students or higher-grade elementary students could provide a valuable peer-tutoring program.

Provide all students with an organizer for keeping track of assignments. Schedule time at the end of each day for the use of this organizational tool. If needed, work cooperatively with parents by maintaining a homework book that keeps parents informed regarding homework assignments.

Some schools treat the issue of doing work at home as a privilege that may be withdrawn. The consequence for not completing assignments is that the student must then complete the work at school for five days, after which the student is given another opportunity to demonstrate responsibility for doing homework at home. Note that a supervised school study hall is required. Also, parents must be willing to transport their children when necessary.

**Teasing**

Teasing is great—when it is done properly. Walk into a school staff room or a team's locker room and you will hear lots of it. Teasing helps us all laugh at our own weaknesses and deal with life's little problems. In addition, parents often tease their children, helping them develop a sense of humor and forming a positive bond. Children learn to tease by listening to adults and imitating their actions.

Unfortunately, it is very difficult to learn how to tease in a positive way. You have to be able to understand how the other person feels and avoid comments that might hurt. Avoiding hurtful comments is hard to do because the best teasing is very close to being a "put-down." It is right on the fine line between positive and negative.

Teach children how to tease properly, when to stop, and the importance of apologizing for comments that cross the line. If the teasing is positive, both the teaser and the "teasee" will be laughing. Sometimes, the person being teased does not laugh but does reciprocate by giving a "zinger" right back. That is OK too because it is equal. However, do not allow teasing that is intended to hurt. Such "put-downs" amount to verbal hits.

It is best to think of teasing in three ways and deal with each differently:

*Friendly teasing* is good natured and should be laughed at by both the giver and the receiver. If a child overreacts to this type of teasing, help him or her recognize that no spite was intended. It is important for children to learn to laugh at themselves.

*Incidental teasing* may go a little too far but is not intended to hurt. Teach the child on the receiving end to ignore this type of teasing or to make a statement such as, "Please stop teasing me." If the teasing continues, teach the first child that he or she has gone too far. You may need to teach this message many times, since each situation is different. Remember that the limits on teasing are very abstract and difficult to learn. Children need to receive many teaching messages in many different situations.

*Hurtful teasing* is intended to hurt the other person and should be dealt with as a verbal "hit." Respond with the same clear statement of limits that you use for physical hits. Consider having a "No put-downs!" rule in your home or classroom. Use this phrase whenever you hear the kind of aggressive teasing that is supposed to make someone feel small. Be prepared to enforce your rules. No means no!

## Dishonesty

Most parents and teachers express great frustration when dealing with children who lie and steal. Since the behavior is self-rewarding, any punishments may quickly become excessive, leading to the frequent use of threats with little chance of follow-through. The following is more effective but it is also more difficult and time consuming.

Lying and stealing breach trust. Children only learn the value of trust if you respond accordingly. Whenever children want to do something that involves trust, insist that they be supervised. There is trust in most situations, even when we grant children permission to go alone to the washroom, a place where children frequently throw water or stuff towels in toilets. Having to wait for supervision will quickly convince children of the value of trust. But, here is the key. This method must be done in the matter-of-fact manner of an instructor. You are teaching children the value of trust, not punishing children by removing privileges and making life inconvenient. Simply explain that people who cannot be trusted must be supervised. Someone must be with them to make sure that they behave correctly.

Most children quickly become exasperated with this situation. They begin asking to do things on their own. Then it becomes a teaching situation. Allow them small bits of freedom at first. If they handle themselves correctly, then gradually give more and more. Now they will understand the value of trust.

If the behavior is repeated, you may need to add in a punishment to give the children a very clear message that "No means no!" Just do not rely on punishment as your only response, or children will become sneakier rather than more responsible.

**Disputes**

Small disputes are a common part in the daily lives of children. Too often, adults attempt to referee these spats and end up frustrated and exasperated. When children are very young (under the age of four), adult intervention is often necessary, although it should be done with a minimum of discussion.

By the age of five, most children are quite capable of resolving their own disputes. Try the following sequence whenever children have a conflict that is big enough to require your attention. Start by assigning them to a discussion area such as the kitchen table. Tell them that they must remain there until they work out their problem. When they do, they should come to you, and each must tell you that the problem has been solved. Resist the temptation to ask what solution they came up with. Often, children will reach an understanding that is not easy to explain. Besides, the details of the solution are rarely important.

There is a good reason why each child must tell you that the problem has been solved. Often, one child will attempt to coerce the other with some sort of threat: "If you don't tell Mom that this problem is solved, I'm going to break your favorite toy!" You can usually tell when coercion has occurred. The child who has taken control will usually be the first to tell you that the problem has been solved, so it is important to hear it from the other child as well. Chances are, they will use a different tone of voice and different words. You will hear a very passive, uncertain voice saying, "Yes, I guess it was solved." Tell the first child that you know exactly what occurred, disallow it, and send the child back to finish the task. It is under these circumstances that you may have to monitor the situation and request the details of the resolution.

Remember that children must be taught the skills for handling these problem-solving situations. They do not learn them by accident. Sit with them during the first few times that they are discussing a conflict and teach them exactly what you want them to do. In fact, you may wish to practice the skills before there is an incident, thus decreasing the stress for everyone.

## Tardiness

Behavior management focuses on what to do when students are late. Discipline focuses first on what to do so they will not be late. Here are some guidelines for disciplining tardy students:

- Since students who are late need structure, arrange for another student to meet the tardy student every morning so they can travel to school together.

- Arrange to have someone phone the student each morning to wake him up (with parental permission).

- Provide a school alarm clock.

- Coordinate your efforts with the parents since they have jurisdiction and supervision at home.

- Establish the length of the school day, and have students make up any lost time as well as any missed work.

- If students cannot be relied on to be on time, do not rely on them to handle other situations without supervision. It is logical for irresponsible attitudes regarding punctuality to influence decisions about students' ability to handle other situations and privileges in school.

- When students are deliberately late, ensure that any missed work is completed. You may even want to have them redo opening exercises to give the message that their behavior will not work. Since their behavior amounts to deliberate defiance, you may find it necessary to attach a consequence in an effort to give the students a clear message. Ensure that the consequence is not presented as a choice. (This is the reason students are sometimes suspended for being late or for skipping school. Although a suspension does not appear to make sense under the circumstances, it is actually a response to the defiance, not to the tardiness or absence.)

**Off-Task Behavior**

There are many reasons why children repeatedly go off task. Usually, the cause can be determined through objective observation by the teacher. When ADD is being considered, however, remember that only medical personnel can make this diagnosis, although teacher observations can be very useful. Teachers are usually very insightful at differentiating the extent to which a student cannot stay on task, as opposed to choosing not to stay on task. ADD behaviors are dealt with in chapter 25. Note that inconsistent home routines, inadequate sleep, and poor nutrition have a significant impact on students, decreasing attention, self-control, and motivation. Where possible, work with parents to improve their decision making in these areas.

In general, students who are off task need to be directed back on task. Direct them nonverbally whenever possible in order to avoid drawing undue attention to the students. Nonverbal prompts and cues also help the teacher avoid personal disruption of their lessons.

Use the power of physical proximity, which can significantly limit the tendency of students to be off task. Either stand next to students or move their desks to a location close to where you normally stand in the classroom. Do not make the movement of the desk a consequence of misbehavior. You should be indicating that it is being moved to prevent problems, not in response to problems.

Some simply wish to avoid the task and would rather socialize or play. Use "Grandma's rule" by requiring low-interest tasks to be completed prior to the start of high-interest tasks ("You can watch television as soon as your homework is done"). Note that this strategy creates a sequence (first things first) rather than giving an "if ... then ..." choice.

Students who are easily distracted may need to be provided with a quiet place to work. Provide this quiet place as a positive study skill, not as a punishment. Also, keep interruptions to a minimum, including teacher interruptions. When students are assigned tasks that they perceive to be mundane, many of them will shift their attention to more interesting alternatives. As much as possible, design activities to capture students' attention. Stress "hands-on" involvement. Provide opportunities for student choice. Show personal enthusiasm for the lesson. Try having them "beat the clock."

Children often respond with off-task behavior when they are assigned tasks that are beyond their abilities, or when the length of the task exceeds the students' ability to maintain concentration. Hence, it is important to design tasks to match the ability levels of students. Also, recognize that people increasingly "multitask," and the skill of sustained attention for a single task is decreasing throughout society. Make sure you present work in short, intense "chunks." Insert quizzes and drills in your lessons. Vary the nature of the activities. When assigning tasks, ensure that students understand the assignment by having them repeat your directions. Use proximity to help keep the students on task. Also, use task-focused questions to keep them engaged with their work ("What question are you on now?).

## Learned Helplessness

Many of our teaching efforts with learning disabled and underachieving students are focused on assisting them to achieve success in their work based on the belief that "success breeds success." Thus, we frequently provide these students with significant amounts of extra attention and assistance, either through the services of learning resource teachers or by enrolling the students in special classes with lower pupil-teacher ratios.

Unfortunately, many students do not benefit from this extra assistance, to the point where they become mastery-oriented learners. Instead, they remain dependent on adults throughout their school careers. Research on attribution (To what do you attribute your success or failure?) has demonstrated some of the causes for this dependency, and the results have significant implications for education. The research suggests that success only breeds success when learners attribute their success to personal effort or ability. If learners attribute the success to factors outside of themselves, such as the teacher, the extra assistance, the easier book, the different type of examination, and so on, a dependency cycle will be initiated. Within this cycle, the learner becomes reliant on outside influences and believes that personal effort will not have a positive influence on the outcome of the task. At the same time, learned helpless students frequently attribute failure experiences to themselves, leading to low self-esteem and a self-sustaining cycle of failure and underachievement.

There are two important solutions to this problem. First, students must be taught to attribute their successes to their personal hard work. Research shows that such retraining is possible. Teach students to make comments to themselves such as "I got it because I didn't give up." "If I keep trying, I'm sure I will be able to do it." "I got it all by myself."

The second key is to recognize that teachers are generally responsible for helping students get "unstuck" whenever the students feel they are unable to go any further. For the students to be successful, they are the ones who must own the strategies for getting unstuck.

To understand this concept, simply look at how you would handle this type of situation personally. When you were taking university or college courses and could not do an assignment, what did you do? Chances are you did not wait around for the instructor. To receive help from the instructor, you would probably have to arrange an appointment time, and one might not be available for several days. Rather than wait, you immediately considered your options. You could contact someone else who was working on the same assignment, talk to someone who previously took the course, or go to the library and find additional books on the subject. No matter which course of action you chose, you were in charge of getting yourself unstuck. You did not have to rely on anyone else to tell you what you should do.

It is important for students to have the same skills. Hence, when students tell you that they are stuck, do not be too quick to give them directions. First, ask them what they have done to get unstuck. If necessary, tape a list of possible solutions to each student's desk. Make sure that they try to problem-solve it themselves before you provide directions.

## Resistance to Change

Everyone resists change (including teachers), even when it would make life easier or more successful in the long run. People want a certain level of predictability in the world around them because it provides a sense of security. Students are no different.

Structure your expectation for change in small and realistic steps. In cooperation with the students, set reasonable and finite goals. Provide feedback on the students' efforts as they work toward their goals. Acknowledge the students' efforts and commitment, particularly when they succeed in overcoming obstacles. Use shared rewards because they encourage peers to actively support each other's efforts. Shared rewards also serve to raise a student's status within a peer group, a situation that can have a dramatic positive effect on the student.

Anticipate that students will experience setbacks. Avoid overreacting. Reset the goals, and demonstrate confidence in the students' ability to get back on track. Remember that people are more willing to accept the risks associated with behavioral change when other aspects of their lives are stable and successful. You can anticipate a high level of resistance from students whose lives are chaotic and who feel inadequate in coping with daily events.

## Problems with Rotary

In the early school years, children have a distinct need for the formation of positive relationships with significant adults. Hence, at these levels, most schools implement a structure which ensures that children interact with one teacher for the majority of the school day. As students mature, they become increasingly capable of handling variations within the learning environment, including increased subject specialization and the resulting rotary schedule.

Whereas some students demonstrate this level of maturity early on, others may require considerably more time and experience. For these students, an extensive rotary schedule may conflict with their developmental needs, resulting in dysfunctional behavior such as a lack of productivity, disruptiveness, and a lack of personal responsibility. Many of these problems can be prevented by ensuring that a school's rotary structure is designed to meet the developmental needs of students. Below are some guidelines:

- Provide a homeroom base with a teacher who takes responsibility for the guidance and counseling of a group of students, as well as making decisions that relate personal needs to learning needs. The teacher should maintain close contact with each student in the group and follow each student's progress.

- Establish a system of communication that keeps the homeroom teacher apprised of each student's behavior in rotary subjects.

- Include the teaching of organizational skills in the homeroom timetable. Design the rotary schedule to ensure that students return to their homerooms at the end of each day and receive assistance in organizing themselves relative to homework and other responsibilities.

- Establish appropriate limits on the use of rotary in order to ensure that each student has the opportunity to maintain the positive personal relationship with the homeroom teacher that fulfills an important developmental need.

- Whenever possible, include students in discussions regarding academic and social progress in order to encourage them to assume personal responsibility and ownership.

# Tip of the Week

Get Your "Tip of the Week" at www.realdiscipline.com

Contact the author by email at morrish@iaw.on.ca
or through Woodstream Publishing
PO Box 1093
Fonthill, Ontario, Canada L0S 1E0
Phone: 905-892-2715 Fax: 905-892-8936

# Recommended Reading

Curwin, Richard, and Allen Mendler. 1988. *Discipline with dignity.*
  Alexandria, VA: Association for Supervision and Curriculum
  Development.
  ISBN 0-87120-154-2

Ramsey, Robert. 1994. *Administrator's complete school discipline
  guide: Techniques and materials for creating an environment where
  kids can learn.* Englewood Cliffs, NJ: Prentice Hall.
  ISBN 0-13-079401-5

Wong, Harry, and Rosemary Wong. 1998. *The first days of school:
  How to be an effective teacher.* Mountain View, CA: Harry K.
  Wong Publications Inc.
  ISBN 0-9629360-2-2

# Appendix A

The following worksheets may be employed to support your efforts at developing school discipline. Please feel free to modify them in any way.

**Develop a Common Vision**

How do you want the students at your school to behave?
In what ways is this different from their behavior outside of the school?
Which of their present behaviors should be blocked? (Not here!)
What skills and attitudes must be taught to the students?
Where is the staff in terms of teamwork?
What obstacles must be overcome in order to achieve the desired results?

| DECIDE HOW YOUR STUDENTS WILL BEHAVE | |
|---|---|
| **Courtesy** | |
| · How will your students speak to you? What tone of voice will they use? | |
| · When you greet them, will they respond in kind? | |
| · How will they speak to other students and to other teachers? | |
| · Will they hold doors open for others? | |
| · How will they treat visitors? | |
| · Do you expect to hear "please" and "thank you" from them? | |
| · Will they be welcoming to new students? | |
| · How will they behave when another student is making a presentation to the class? | |
| · Will they listen when you are speaking? | |
| · Will they wait patiently when you are speaking to others? | |

# DECIDE HOW YOUR STUDENTS WILL BEHAVE

| | |
|---|---|
| **Response to Frustration**<br><br>· What will they do when they are upset?<br><br>· How will they disagree with you or others?<br><br>· How will they handle a failing grade?<br><br>· How will they deal with losing? | |
| **Treatment of Others**<br><br>· How will your students behave for substitute teachers?<br><br>· How will they treat students who are new to the school?<br><br>· How will they treat visitors?<br><br>· How will they respond to students who need assistance? | |
| **Response to Authority**<br><br>· How will your students respond when you correct them?<br><br>· Will they comply when you tell them what to do?<br><br>· How will they respond to directions from a teacher who is not "one of theirs"? | |
| **Situations**<br><br>· How will they behave when you step out of the room or have your back turned, or when you are busy helping an individual or working with a group?<br><br>· How will they conduct themselves during assemblies? | |

# DECIDE HOW YOUR STUDENTS WILL BEHAVE

| | |
|---|---|
| **Work Habits**<br><br>· Will your students complete their assignments?<br><br>· Will they work up to their potential?<br><br>· Will they willingly improve their work if it is deemed sub-standard?<br><br>· How will they deal with mundane tasks? | |
| **Cooperative Play**<br><br>· Will your students accept others into their games?<br><br>· Will they *invite* others into their games?<br><br>· How will they handle "getting out" in a game?<br><br>· Will they share items with other students? | |

| BUILDING SCHOOL DISCIPLINE Developing an Action Plan | | | |
|---|---|---|---|
| Issue | Action | Person/People Responsible | Time Line |
| Blocking of incompatible behaviors | | | |
| Schoolwide structure, routines, and procedures | | | |
| Schoolwide training camp | | | |
| Supervision requirements | | | |
| Developing teacher authority | | | |
| Teaching of skills and attitudes | | | |
| Motivational tools | | | |
| Appropriate use of consequences | | | |
| Improving staff teamwork | | | |

| Issue | Action | Person/People Responsible | Time Line |
|---|---|---|---|
| Schoolwide consistency | | | |
| Standards | | | |
| Continuous progress | | | |
| Leadership | | | |
| Building the parent partnership | | | |
| Quality of regular program | | | |
| Making discipline part of the school culture | | | |
| Invitational nature of school | | | |
| School equipment and activities | | | |
| Overcoming identified obstacles | | | |

# Appendix B

**Behavioral Continuum**
**(Scope and Sequence)**
**Kindergarten through Grade 8**

Here is a challenge that has just begun. One hundred teachers worked on developing this continuum. One of the most difficult aspects involved selecting the categories (compliance, cooperation, etc.). Several very different formats were considered, and each one of them had advantages and disadvantages when compared to the rest (just one of the reasons for suggesting that this effort has just begun).

The process for developing the continuum was fairly straightforward. A group of kindergarten teachers determined the skills that they could teach their students, presuming the students had arrived a school with a reasonable foundation already developed at home. Grade 1 teachers were then shown the responses from the kindergarten teachers. The question to them was this, "Assuming the kindergarten teachers accomplish what they have indicated, what would the students be able to do with one more year of training? Once these answers were received, the grade 2 teachers added in their responses, and so on up to Grade 8.

The overall effect was fascinating. The accumulation of skills across the grades created extraordinarily high expectations and skill levels. Many teachers found it difficult to believe what the teachers before them had determined. However, they consistently said that if the previous teachers could produce such great results, then they could certainly go even further. These results, of course, demonstrate the power of building skills across the grades.

As you read these charts, your first reaction may be that such an accomplishment this would be impossible. However, every school has a number of great students who already behave this way. Now, we need to systematically teach the rest to do likewise.

# Compliance (Respect for Rules)

| Kindergarten | Grade 5 |
|---|---|
| Learn classroom routines<br>Follow teacher directions | Comply for the right reasons<br>Understand rationale for rules |
| **Grade 1**<br>Follow rules for playground, recess, and lunch<br>Require fewer adults on trips<br>Comply with teacher designates | **Grade 6**<br>Are expected to serve as models for younger students<br>Reach consensus through discussion<br>Take ownership<br>Suggest extra rules |
| **Grade 2**<br>Comply with and assist teacher designates | **Grades 7 and 8**<br>Differentiate between positive and negative leadership |
| **Grade 3**<br>Comply with students who are designated as group leaders | Adjust to new school situation and new peers (where appropriate)<br>Comply without excessive supervision<br>Handle rules applied flexibly |
| **Grade 4**<br>Comply despite negative peer pressure | |

# Participation

| Kindergarten | Grade 4 |
|---|---|
| Develop comfort level for contributing<br>Take turns<br>Build routines<br>Are active and passive | Are independent, need no coaxing<br>Volunteer<br>Join in a variety of activities, not just favorites |
| **Grade 1**<br>Raise hands<br>Are a good audience<br>Know routines<br>Are on topic and make meaningful comments | **Grade 5**<br>Have an opinion that they want heard<br>Are more reflective |
| **Grade 2**<br>Participate in group discussions<br>Stay on task<br>Are a good audience | **Grade 6**<br>Debate issues<br>Are able to take opposite sides<br>Confident about personal beliefs<br>Participate with "ears" |
| **Grade 3**<br>Are able to present to group comfortably<br>Are able to have small group discussions and reach common answer<br>Have more confidence in individual answers | **Grades 7 and 8**<br>Develop and present informed opinions<br>Back up belief statements<br>Question personal beliefs |

# Cooperation

| Kindergarten | Grade 4 |
|---|---|
| Play with others<br>Show tolerance<br>Avoid problems with one another<br>Are teacher directed | Offer assistance to others |
| | **Grade 5** |
| | Accomodate others<br>Develop citizenship (understand community needs)<br>Develop people and leadership skills |
| **Grade 1** | |
| Play with others<br>Show tolerance<br>Avoid problems with one another<br>Are child directed | |
| | **Grade 6** |
| | Accept other students as leaders<br>Build on strengths of others and compensate for weaknesses |
| **Grade 2** | |
| Refine skills<br>Apply them independently | |
| | **Grades 7 and 8** |
| **Grade 3** | Are more empathetic<br>Appreciate others |
| Are able to work in small groups<br>Think of others<br>Are willing helpers | Are sympathetic to people who struggle<br>Rally around, solve problems of others and world problems |

# Collaboration

| Kindergarten | Grade 5 |
|---|---|
| **Grade 1** | Work in larger groups<br>Structure roles<br>Take turns doing roles<br>Use personal strengths<br>Evaluate self |
| Perform assigned tasks<br>Perform academic tasks<br>Are teacher directed | |
| **Grade 2** | **Grade 6** |
| Are beginning cooperative learning (teacher directed) | Initiate collaboration as required for tasks<br>Recognize and build on capabilities of others<br>Problem-solve handling weaknesses |
| **Grade 3** | **Grades 7 and 8** |
| Require less teacher direction for collaborative learning | Move away from traditional groups<br>Do not just work with friends<br>Pick people for a specific purpose |
| **Grade 4** | Change groupings as tasks change<br>Insist that all students pull their weight |
| Work with any student in the class | Recognize need to delegate tasks<br>Evaluate others in group (peer evaluation) |

# Accountability

| Kindergarten | Grade 4 |
|---|---|
| Clean up after self | Demonstrate ownership of group actions |
| | Apply to situations that are more complex |
| **Grade 1** | Keep appointments and commitments |
| Complete work to capability | |
| Carry out assigned classroom tasks with teacher direction | **Grade 5** |
| | Are more dependable—teacher reminders not required |
| **Grade 2** | Listen for announcements affecting self |
| Demonstrate personal sense of best effort in work | |
| Perceive school class as a community | **Grade 6** |
| | Need very few reminders |
| **Grade 3** | **Grades 7 and 8** |
| Take care of group area | Continue with needing very few reminders |
| Have a sense of community | Track personal responsibilities and tasks |
| Complete jobs independently | Prepare self for school day and individual classes |
| | Organize self and work |
| | Plan and schedule effectively |

# Conflict Management

| Kindergarten | Grade 4 |
|---|---|
| Are teacher directed | Resolve problems that are more complex |
| Learn beginning routines | Handle increasing negative peer pressure |
| Inform adults rather than tattling | |
| | **Grade 5** |
| **Grade 1** | Continue as per grade 4 |
| Discuss problems with other students | Put oneself "in the shoes of others" |
| Learn to express feelings | |
| Respond to feelings of others | **Grade 6** |
| | Extend skills |
| **Grade 2** | Analyze situations |
| Use discussions with other students to find solutions to problems | Plan ways to avoid conflicts |
| | Apply self-restraint |
| **Grade 3** | **Grades 7 and 8** |
| Refine solutions | Know when to seek support from peers, counselors, agencies, etc. |
| Find sensible solutions | Seek out ways to resolve conflict |
| Suggest appropriate consequences | Manage stress by reducing it to personal advantage |
| Select peer mediator | |

# Self-Discipline

| Kindergarten | Grade 4 |
|---|---|
| Maintain behavior for 5 minutes while teacher works with group or leaves room | Maintain behavior for 30–40 minutes while teacher is busy<br>Maintain behavior for a minimum of 30 minutes without direct supervision* |
| **Grade 1**<br>Maintain behavior for 10 minutes while teacher is busy<br>Maintain behavior for 5 minutes without direct supervision* | **Grade 5**<br>Maintain behavior (limited by length of periods)<br>Maintain behavior for 40 minutes without direct supervision* |
| **Grade 2**<br>Maintain behavior for 15 minutes while teacher is busy<br>Maintain behavior for 7–10 minutes without direct supervision* | **Grade 6**<br>Maintain behavior (limited by length of periods)<br>Maintain behavior for 40 minutes without direct supervision* |
| **Grade 3**<br>Maintain behavior for 20–30 minutes while teacher is busy<br>Maintain behavior for 10–30 min. without direct supervision* | **Grades 7 and 8**<br>Work until task is complete or time limit is reached<br>Take personal short breaks as required without interfering with the work of other students |

\* In the library or when teacher leaves
    the room

# Organization/Time Management

| Kindergarten and Grade 1 | Grade 5 |
|---|---|
| Follow teacher models for organization<br>Respond to notification that time is almost up<br>Choose and complete free-time activities for limited times | Get started on own<br>Take on new projects that continue for 5–7 periods (teacher helps organize and structure)<br>Need less supervision |
| **Grade 2**<br>Plan for the use of time for half of the day | |
| **Grade 3**<br>Plan for the use of time for a full day<br>Finish incomplete work | **Grade 6**<br>Prioritize lists of tasks, allocate time required, and pace self<br>Negotiate time to complete tasks<br>Use schedules, etc. |
| **Grade 4**<br>Complete personal planners<br>Use spare time to finish other tasks<br>Have good study habits<br>Complete homework | **Grades 7 and 8**<br>Continue as before<br>Have ability to keep appointments |

# Perseverance

| | |
|---|---|
| **Kindergarten**<br>Stay on task for 10–20 minutes, including listening time | **Grade 4**<br>Accomplish more or better work during 60 minutes |
| **Grade 1**<br>Work on task a maximum of 30 minutes, depending on structure and active nature of task | **Grade 5**<br>Accomplish more or better work during 60 minutes |
| **Grade 2**<br>Work on task for 30–60 minutes, depending on degree of structure and active nature of task | **Grade 6**<br>Accomplish tasks that are increasingly self-directed<br>Use time effectively |
| **Grade 3**<br>Work on task for 60 minutes, with short breaks (self-directed, including return to task)<br>Meet more complex demands | **Grades 7 and 8**<br>Complete tasks despite decreasing motivation and decreasing desire to please teacher |

# Independence

| | |
|---|---|
| **Kindergarten**<br>Separate from Mom<br>Dress and undress self<br>Take care of personal belongings<br>Establish washroom routines<br>Play on own<br>Transition | **Grade 4**<br>Select teams and games<br>Suggest own activities<br>Advocate for personal rights<br>Disagree in appropriate manner |
| **Grade 1**<br>Do academic work<br>Bring items from home<br>Follow classroom routines<br>Find constructive activities from list | **Grade 5**<br>Start to question rules and directions<br>Learn to compromise<br>Design work to suit personal interests and make suggestions for learning activities |
| **Grade 2**<br>Read and follow instructions<br>Are responsible for items sent home<br>Are totally responsible for items for school | **Grade 6**<br>Self-evaluate previous choices and outcomes<br>Adjust choices accordingly<br>Organize activities<br>Extend questioning of rules (fairness) |
| **Grade 3**<br>Complete work<br>Do research, bring back information to class<br>Attend intermurals<br>Find constructive activities on own | **Grades 7 and 8**<br>Consolidate skills<br>Apply skills to more complex situations<br>Assess personal strengths and weaknesses<br>Advocate for rights of others and social concerns |

# Appendix C

The following guidelines were developed and adopted by the Lincoln County Board of Education in St. Catharines, Ontario, Canada. Permission to reprint the guidelines has been granted by the District School Board of Niagara, which was formed by merging the Lincoln County Board of Education and the Niagara South Board of Education.

The guidelines were designed to govern the conduct of educational personnel. They offer clear and unequivocal support for professional actions undertaken in the best interests of children, while rejecting actions that would be considered punitive.

All aspects of the guidelines were developed in cooperation with legal personnel. In addition, support was received from all major social agencies, including Family and Children's Services that deals with child protection.

## Lincoln County Board of Education
(Now the District School Board of Niagara)

### Physical Intervention Procedures and Guidelines

PREAMBLE

The Lincoln County Board of Education is committed to the goal that all students should learn to be responsible, cooperative and productive individuals. To this end, the Board supports the use of instructional and disciplinary techniques that are designed to teach the skills and attitudes that students require in order to function effectively within society. In particular, preventative intervention, the positive reinforcement of desired behaviors, and the development of social skills and conflict resolution strategies are considered the most useful tools for promoting growth and development.

## SECTION A: STANDARD PHYSICAL INTERVENTION PROCEDURES

The Board recognizes that effective instruction and discipline occasionally require physical contact between staff and students. This includes contact that occurs as an integral part of the learning process. It also includes contact that is used by staff to facilitate a student's performance of a desired behavior. Such contact is considered appropriate provided that it reflects the constructive nature of effective teaching and discipline techniques. Examples include, but are not limited to, contact that occurs when:

1. a student is being praised or rewarded.
2. a staff member is attempting to establish or improve rapport during work sessions, play periods or counseling.
3. role playing is being employed for the teaching of social skills or problem resolution.
4. a student requires assistance for the learning of a specific skill (e.g. printing, using school equipment, learning physical education skills, etc.)
5. a student requires assistance for improving attention to task.
6. a student requires assistance for the control of excessive body movements.
7. maintenance exercises are undertaken for physiotherapy and occupational therapy.
8. nonverbal cues (such as taps to the hand, shoulder, etc.) are employed as a means of assisting a student to recognize misbehavior, improve self-control and avoid disciplinary procedures.
9. a student requires assistance in following directions from staff to move from one location to another (in the absence of significant student resistance).
10. a student requires assistance in following directions from staff to release an object in his or her possession (in the absence of significant student resistance).

**Note:** These categories and examples of appropriate physical contact are not intended to be exhaustive. The use of physical contact in other situations would also be considered appropriate, provided that the contact clearly reflects the positive philosophy and constructive nature of effective teaching and discipline techniques.

## SECTION B: INTENSIVE PHYSICAL INTERVENTION PROCEDURES

The Board recognizes that some students display a level of inappropriate behavior that is not always controllable or alterable by the use of standard school disciplinary procedures. Therefore, the use of intensive intervention techniques may be required in order to achieve a productive resolution of the behavioral difficulties. These techniques include the use of physical contact to a greater extent than would normally be employed and physical restraint where concerns for the safety of students and staff justify the use of this procedure. As with standard school disciplinary procedures, the use of such techniques should reflect the philosophy that the primary aim of discipline is for all students to acquire the positive skills and attitudes associated with responsible conduct.

### INTENSIVE PHYSICAL CONTACT

This includes contact that may occur when:
1. staff is required to intercede in a dispute between students.
2. a student requires assistance in following directions from staff to move from one location to another (with significant student resistance).
3. a student requires assistance in following directions from staff to release an object in his or her possession (with significant student resistance).
4. the staff member uses a self-protection release or block as a means of avoiding personal injury caused by aggressive student behavior.

### Guidelines for Intensive Physical Contact

1. Intensive physical contact must be employed with caution. The deliberate overuse of force such that a student is shaken violently, pulled in a strong jerking manner, struck punitively, etc. is forbidden.
2. To ensure that these techniques are used in a visibly constructive manner, the staff member should maintain personal self-control and composure throughout the application.
3. When a student is being moved or is required to release an object, it may be necessary to enlist the aid of another staff member so that the desired goal may be achieved without hurting the student.
4. Intensive physical contact must not be employed punitively or

threatened in such a way that it would likely be perceived as a punishment.

5. Other students should not be enlisted by staff for assistance in the use of intensive physical contact. It is recognized that students may voluntarily become involved in certain situations, such as intervening in a dispute between other students.

## PHYSICAL RESTRAINT

Physical restraint refers to a preventative procedure used when there is a realistic concern that a student may suffer personal injury, injure others or cause significant property damage. Due to the intrusive nature of physical restraint, the Board expects staff to limit the use of this procedure to those situations that are not resolvable by other disciplinary procedures.

In addition, the Board expects staff to use early intervention strategies whenever possible to prevent a situation from escalating to the point where physical restraint would be required. Early intervention includes the recognition of a student's early symptoms of anxiety. During this phase, a supportive and empathic approach by staff may defuse or de-escalate the potential crisis. Students who escalate beyond the anxiety level may display defensive behavior and a loss of rational control. During this phase, staff should maintain a controlled and professional manner while setting behavioral limits that are clear, concise and enforceable. Approaches such as these may reduce likelihood that a student will escalate to the level of aggressive and assaultive behavior that may require physical restraint.

Mechanical Devices: Various mechanical devices are available which could be employed to restrict a student's freedom of movement. The Board supports the use of those devices which are intended to ensure the physical safety of students from accidental or self-directed injury. Examples of such devices include straps or belts to prevent students from falling out of chairs or wheelchairs, standing frames, protective equipment for students with seizures, seatbelts, and equipment designed to prevent self-injury.

The Board does *not* support the use of mechanical restraint devices for *disciplinary action*. Examples include, but are not limited to, straps or belts used to forcibly confine or restrict a student, and the use of tape or any other object to restrict a child's ability to speak. Neither does the Board support the isolation of a student in a locked room except in emergency circumstances. Under these circumstances, the student must be observed and supervised by staff and an Incident Report Form must be completed.

## Guidelines for Physical Restraint

1. Physical restraint is a safety procedure employed to protect people and property. It must not be applied as a punishment.
2. To ensure that these techniques are used in a visibly constructive manner, the staff member should attempt to maintain personal self-control and composure throughout the application.
3. Physical restraint must be employed with caution. The deliberate overuse of force such that a student is shaken violently, pulled in a strong jerking manner, struck punitively etc. is forbidden.
4. Restraint may be employed to confine a student within the classroom or school under circumstances where the student has demonstrated a desire or willingness to leave a supervised area without permission such that his or her personal safety could be jeopardized. This procedure would also apply during school trips and excursions.
5. When applying restraint, staff must use only the minimum amount of force required for the protection of people and property. It may be necessary to enlist the aid of another staff member to the holding session so that control may be achieved without hurting the student.
6. Staff may counsel students to help them understand how their actions could escalate to a restraint situation. However, restraint must not be used as a threat.
7. Other students must not be involved in the application of physical restraint.
8. Throughout any restraint, staff should reassure the student that restraint is being used for reasons of safety until the student regains self-control. Under circumstances where such communication could intensify the student's emotional outburst, the staff may choose to reassure the student after self-control has been recovered.
9. Appropriate follow-up should occur subsequent to the use of physical

restraint in an effort to resolve conflict and avoid the need to utilize physical restraint in the future. This may include recognition of feelings, counseling, the discussion of alternative courses of action, role-playing where appropriate and an attempt at resolution through mutual goal setting.

### Physical Restraint Procedures

The Board recognizes that one-person restraints are the accepted norm in school-based programs due to staffing limitations and the traditional classroom design of schools. Therefore, although two-person restraints may be preferable and are easier to perform, the Board authorizes staff to use one-person restraints when required to protect the safety and security of students and staff.

### One-Person Restraint:

The preferred methods for one-person physical restraint include:

(a) "Wrap-Around Hold": The student is seated on a chair or on the floor with the staff standing or sitting behind the student. The student's arms are crossed in front and the staff holds the student's wrists.

(b) "Basket Hold" or "Cradle Hold": In this hold, the student is in a semi-prone, face-up position set sideways to the staff member and is "cradled" in the staff member's arms. This hold is only appropriate for very young students, but is very useful because of the security that it provides. To move a student into this hold, the student's arm which is nearest to the staff member is wrapped across the student's chest and over the student's far shoulder with the wrist held by the staff member. The student's other arm is also held by the wrist with the arm positioned under the student's knees.

(c) "Straddle Hold": When necessary, the staff member may straddle or sit on a student providing precautions are taken to ensure that excessive weight is not applied to the student's lower spine area ('small' of the back) or any other area clearly prone to injury. The student's wrists are held with the arms being (1) at the student's sides, (2) across the student's back with the hands meeting in the small of the back, or

(3) across the student's back with the hands overlapping at a point approximately midway up the back. These three arm positions should be considered a progression in terms of restrictiveness with staff using no greater restriction than is required for control.

## Two-Person Restraint:

The preferred method for two-person physical restraint is:

Staff members face the same direction. They place their inside legs in front of the student. Staff members' outside hands hold the student's wrists with the student's hands rotated to a palms-up position. Staff members' inside hands are positioned on the student's shoulders.

**Note:** Whereas these methods for One-Person and Two-Person Restraint are preferred, it is recognized that modifications of these procedures may be necessary depending upon the nature and severity of the problem. Such modifications would be appropriate provided they continue to reflect the overall concerns regarding safety and nonpunitive control.

## Reporting Procedures

When physical restraint has been employed, the following procedures are to be followed:

1. A "Physical Restraint Incident Report" (Appendix Form #1) must be completed and submitted to the Principal of the school within one school day of the incident. This form shall be made available to the parents or guardians upon request.
2. The parents or guardians of the student must be notified that the restraint has been employed. Notification may be in person, by phone, or by regular mail. A sample letter is attached to these procedures (Appendix Form #2). Please note, however, that the Board encourages personal contact with parents whenever possible.
   It is not recommended that students be required to carry this information home either in the form of a letter or as a note written in a "Communication Book." These methods increase the likelihood that the notification would be discarded in transit, thereby creating additional problems which could have been avoided.

3. For students enrolled in specialized programs, such as Behavioral Adjustment, parents or guardians should be informed during the initial intake meeting that intensive intervention procedures may be employed, including physical restraint. The parents or guardians then sign a copy of the Notification form (Appendix Form #3), acknowledging that they have been informed of these procedures.

### Alternative Reporting Procedures:

It is recognized that a few students experience such significant difficulties that physical restraint must be used on a frequent basis. In such cases, the staff may choose to employ a "log" which provides a record of all relevant information regarding each incident. Staff is not required to notify the student's parents or guardians after each incident. The following procedures and restrictions apply to the use of these alternative reporting procedures:

1. This procedure should only be implemented for students who demonstrate specific repetitive behaviors that predictably escalate to aggressive and injurious levels.
2. The parents or guardians of the student must be fully informed about the use of alternative reporting procedures. A parental acknowledgment form is included in the appendix (Appendix Form #4).
3. A separate log must be maintained for each student. Logs must include the following information: Date, Time, Duration, Location, Restraint technique employed, the name of each staff member directly involved in the restraint. (Additional information may be added at the discretion of staff.)
4. This log must be shared with the parents or guardians upon their request.
5. Staff should continue to complete a full Incident Report and use notification procedures whenever an incident involves new or unusually severe behaviors.